French Dreams, Dogs and a Dodgy Motor

Jane Smyth

Contents

Chapter 1
HOW IT ALL STARTED

I have always loved curling up with a good book, losing myself in the story, whether real or imagined, tragic or happy. I have laughed and cried; some stories have stayed with me to this day while others faded away almost as soon as I closed the covers. This love of a good read was encouraged from a very early age by my mum who, working full time in Birmingham, used to head into Hudson's bookstore in the city centre every Thursday (payday) and buy a book for me and one for my elder brother. By the age of ten, I had read all the children's classics and, like most kids of my generation, became totally besotted by Enid Blyton and her endless tales of adventure, mystery or schoolgirl shenanigans.

Even after marriage when children started arriving, I always had a book ready to spend a few quiet minutes with to escape the endless stream of dirty nappies and housework. The towelling variety needed soaking, washing and drying outdoors on a daily basis. Tumble dryers were rare and disposable nappies had yet to be invented!

I was also juggling the demands of two small children and running the home, often by myself, as my hard-working husband was frequently called away because of his job. Later, a part-time job followed, running alongside my studies to become a teacher. Reading a book for pleasure became non-existent for a while as I ploughed through the demands of educational psychology and spent hours writing long, detailed essays and prepared lessons for teaching practice.

Eventually, a full-time lecturing position and a salary meant that we could now go 'abroad' for holidays and for many years, while the kids were growing up, we headed to France on camping trips. Rob had also secured a good job working for an international company that took him to many far-flung destinations around the world, paid him a reasonable salary and, wonderfully, provided him with a new company car every three years.

We'd never had a new car, spending our early married life with a series of old bangers in various states of decay. Indeed, when in labour with our daughter, Rob rushed me to hospital in our Mini that, prior to our ownership, had been subjected to several complete repaint jobs. We only knew this because there were so many chips and scratches on the bodywork all previous attempts at colour improvement were beginning to reveal themselves. Currently, the overall colour was a shade of pale green with patches of rusty metalwork. It also had unreliable gears. The car objected to third gear in particular by kicking it back into neutral whilst in transit and worryingly, also had a hole in the floor on the passenger side through which the surface of the road could be seen, passing by in a blur as we raced along. I couldn't have cared less. At this point, my labour pains were hitting me in waves about five minutes apart. Neither did I care when Rob went the wrong way around a traffic island. Well, it was 3.30 am in the morning with no one about and, bless him, he was in rather a panic.

Our first new car arrived. A beautiful Ford Cortina MkII in dark blue with a light blue interior. It had that wonderful new car smell and blemish-free bodywork. The gears stayed put and didn't move of their own accord. It was deemed a 'limo' and stayed that way until the next new 'limo' came into our lives three years later. Rob and I could now start planning the first of our trips abroad in our new car, accompanied by our two young children – our daughter having now been joined by a brother, two and a half years her junior.

The trip involved driving through France and into northern Spain. We had booked it through a tour company that planned the itinerary and set tight arrival times at stopovers in a series of grotty hotels. That was also the year in which all ferries were diverted to Ostend because of a French fishermen's blockade resulting in an horrendous journey of ten hours to the first of the overnight stops. Amazingly, this didn't dampen our enthusiasm for what became regular road trips around France. For years, we spent our summer holidays under canvas, having dragged a variety of tents in trailers to every corner of the country. Our kids loved it and so did we.

We loved the culture, the quiet roads and the stunning scenery, not least the amazing gastronomy. The seeds of what we considered an impossible dream were gradually taking root.

Back to reading... I've always loved autobiographies, basically because I'm really nosey, and as by now I'd morphed into a committed Francophile, a book combining these two loves was guaranteed to attract my attention. When *A Year in Provence* by the late Peter Mayle, was published in 1989, like millions of others, I read it, loved it and fantasised about becoming the owner of a house just like his. In my mind's eye, I could see Rob and me sitting beside a glittering blue pool sipping a cool glass of wine. The garden would be filled with the sound of chirping cicadas and as the sun slowly slipped below the horizon, the scent of lavender would fill the evening air, carried in on a gentle breeze. A blissful dream of mine, but very much a Provençal cliché and in my case, totally delusional! Rob was as keen as I about buying a property in France and we often spoke about it, but being far more practical, he would generally roll his eyes when I used to dreamily launch into my 'wouldn't it be wonderful if' scenario. His response, delivered with a pinch of humour, would have been something like:

"You're not being realistic. It's never going happen unless some Fairy Godmother or a Genie of the Lamp appears and agrees to grant a wish, and, if I get in first, I just might ask for a Maserati."

"Yeah? Well, you'd never afford the fuel, there'd be no room for the kids and it wouldn't pull our trailer tent! Ha! Now who's being realistic!"

Knowing he was right to pour cold water on my French property-owning fantasies (for now anyway) I temporarily consigned them to the dustbin in my head, and contented myself with simply reading about such delights, devouring Mr Mayles' sequels as soon as they hit the shelves

Dragging my head out of the clouds, it was time to get real; the dream of owning a property in France was simply beyond us back then. We could barely afford the mortgage on our home in the UK, the interest of which, at that point in the 80s, was hovering around the 15% mark, so even a tiny rural shepherd's hut selling for a few hundred pounds was as unlikely as buying a villa on the Riviera or that dreamy Provençal stone house. The seed however stubbornly refused to wither. I continued to feed it by reading all I could, including the rules and practicalities of buying and selling properties in France, the fledgling journals that were cashing in on the popularity of buying such a house, as well as stories detailing the joys, hardships, laughter and tears of those who had actually done it.

They all taught me a lot about buying property in France: the process, the legalities and the laws. I was armed to the teeth with knowledge, just in case we ever found ourselves with enough money. There was a lot of daydreaming and wishful thinking. Perhaps Mum and Dad would win the pools and come to the rescue. They had always promised me a chunk of the winnings if ever it happened. It didn't, except for a win of £90 that they used to buy a carpet. Ernie was no help either as he repeatedly failed to pick my only Premium Bond that I'd had since a child. To this day, he still hasn't managed to find it. Then Lancelot and Guinevere simply refused to spit out our chosen lottery numbers, so we finally gave up trying to persuade Lady Luck to smile upon us. If we were going to realise our dream one day, we needed to rely upon ourselves, and that was going to take a while.

With the advent of E-readers, I discovered a completely new world of people who have told their stories about buying all kinds of French property from grand Chateaux to virtual hovels. Their stories were sometimes inspirational, but exhausting as they described the sheer hard work needed to create the home of their dreams and the struggles encountered along the way with delays, poor building work and bureaucracy. Others left you puzzled at the lack of common sense like, for instance, buying a property for a song but neglecting to pay any attention to the exorbitant costs and timescales involved in major renovation work, ploughing on regardless until either the money or their health gave out and their dream ended up on the scrap heap.

These tales have proven the most educational of all, demonstrating the importance of keeping a level head as you peer through those rose-tinted glasses. For us, any restoration work was a non-starter, especially as we would both be working full time in the UK. We also needed to look closely at where we wanted our future house to be located, what type of property we would consider and what amenities might we want close by. It was a valuable lesson to learn, as the two of us have been guilty of being a tad impulsive on several occasions.

"That's SO nice."

"Can we afford it?"

"No."

"Well maybe ..."

"Oh sod it! Let's go for it!"

This is perhaps forgivable when buying a sound system or TV you can barely afford, but a whole house? Certainly not the time to start throwing caution to the wind!

Most of those who have related their personal stories are not famous authors. They have followed their hearts, picked up the pen or computer keyboard and allowed us a glimpse of their lives as they set forth on their French adventures. Some have been amusing, others heartbreaking. But they've done it and I think I need to say thank you to them all for providing me with sufficient insight on what to do and what not to do when setting out on our own adventure into French property ownership.

Chapter 2
THE CAT GOT AWAY

Whenever I found myself with time on my hands, I often spent it trawling internet sites advertising French properties for sale. It was not with the intention of buying something, it was more a curiosity to see what was out there; a 'What if?' exploration of possibilities and a chance to scrutinize everything from huge Chateaux and enormous villas to derelict houses or rural animal shelters. Being endlessly curious, this virtual world was a place that let me inside properties that were completely out of reach to anyone who was not already in possession of several millions of pounds and a yacht moored in Monaco. I loved peering 'through the keyhole' to see how the other half lived, even knowing that the nearest we'd get to something so luxurious would be on a coach taking tourists for a quick trip past the homes of the rich and famous, with a split-second glance over a security wall or through the bars of some huge ornate gates.

Meanwhile, back on Planet Earth, it soon became obvious that the least expensive homes were either wrecks, or properties in the middle of several square miles of nothingness, surrounded by marshland and mosquitos. As is still the case today, habitable properties could be found all over France, priced according to their location and state of decay. Unfortunately for us, our favourite places were all in the south-east where prices were eye watering for something pretty mundane, or were one of the aforementioned animal shelters requiring an equally eye watering amount of money to knock it into shape! I couldn't help feeling a tad disheartened. Nevertheless, even if buying in France remained a distant dream, there was nothing to lose by looking was there?

Over the years, we did come across people who had managed to find their dream property. In most cases they had 'picked it up for a song'! We met a lovely man who was a member of our French conversation class (more about that later). He and his wife had purchased a cow shed in the Loire; a barn really, but he always referred to it as the cow shed because, surprisingly, it once housed cows. He paid a paltry sum for it. He often brought along to class evidence of the work he was trying to do to turn it into a habitable dwelling. Working full time, he was unable to get there very often and progress was alarmingly slow. He used to joke about how long it would take to finish it. His wife and their two small children usually accompanied him, the whole family living in an old, rather tatty caravan parked on the site. They would toil day after day, often borrowing any heavy equipment they needed from the farmer next door. His children thought the whole thing one big adventure. Regardless of the work, they loved their time there, he'd say, showing us plans of the home of their dreams.

Sadly, we never did find out how far he managed to get with the restoration. Our French class folded after a year or two and we were told a couple of years later that he had passed away. Rob and I were incredibly shocked and saddened. He was such a lovely person, full of funny stories and always happy and positive. Alas, his heart gave out when he was only in his mid-40s. I still wonder what happened to that cow shed and whether his wife ever managed to achieve their dream. I do hope so.

Another conversation regarding the purchase of a French property happened on a cross-channel ferry. What happened next was bizarre. Although not directly involved with the purchase of our property, it demonstrates the sort of trouble you can get yourself into when enjoying a casual chat with strangers.

Cutting a long story short, Rob and I, along with a couple of friends, had been involved in a rather serious car accident in northern France. I totally blame the cat; the one that caused a car travelling in the opposite direction to swerve and hit us. At this point, I would like to reassure all cat lovers that this kamikaze moggy survived intact after its 'chicken' dash across the road, deservedly losing one of its nine lives in the process. We weren't so lucky. Sue and I were hospitalised and the car a complete write-off. My left arm had been badly smashed and the French doctors, rather than carry out any surgery in France, wished me luck with ongoing treatment in the UK, but not before they kindly immobilised my arm against my torso and swaddled me in bandages around my upper body. I really did look like something you would find in an Egyptian sarcophagus, apart from the fact the bandages were clean and I smelled a lot fresher, but more importantly, I was alive and reasonably well.

During my short stay in the hospital, I shared a room with a gorgeous old French lady, whose relatives used to visit each evening but proceeded to spend most of their time with me. Seems our accident had made the local paper and I was somewhat of a celebrity. Obviously, nothing else of consequence occurred in the news that day! My roommate, as lovely as she was, suffered with a bad case of wind which was loudly released on and off during the course of the night. She also snored. Sleep proved a little difficult!

Sue and I were dispatched homewards after a couple of days, both emerging from the hospital; she covered in bruises and me looking ridiculous! The boys, having escaped any injury in the accident were on hand to help, full of joie de vivre after being cared for by the Lion's Club of Caen. Not only had they been given a free hotel room, they had been pampered with some fine dining and had enjoyed a fair amount of alcohol. It was hardly surprising that they were both full of praise for the hospitality and generosity towards two non-members of the organisation. While Sue and I were stuck in our hospital beds, the pair of them had spent a fabulous couple of days, only interrupted by dutiful visits to tell us all about it.

With no transport, but with luggage retrieved, we headed for the ferry port in a taxi. Once aboard, I managed to remain dignified as I wandered into the ferry lounge, ignoring the stares and sniggers as passengers noted my rather odd appearance, my baggy sweatshirt not doing the best of jobs disguising the excessive use of bandaging.

"Oh look Mummy, a mummy!" yelled a small child, laughing.

"Don't point dear, it's rude."

Finding a table and comfortable seats, we started a conversation with a couple seated at the table next to us. Bill and Jen, who informed us they were both teachers, were returning from Brittany after purchasing a farm for £10,000. They were dressed casually in jeans, grimy looking sweatshirts and hairstyles that showed a distinct lack of professional intervention or regular shampooing. Appearances aside, they were both extremely sociable and happy to chat over a few beers, rapturously describing the farm they'd found. Loads of land with a farmhouse which was 'perfect' and 'gorgeous' and 'ready to move into' they explained. We were very sceptical. Habitable homes in this condition were rather more money than they claimed, but who were we to disbelieve them? Perhaps they really had struck lucky.

Arriving in Southampton, we found there were no rental cars available until the following morning, leaving us stranded, so Bill and Jen kindly offered us room and board at their home. We were so in need of a warm bed and a good night's rest that we accepted their offer immediately knowing it saved us the bother of trying to find a hotel. "That's really kind of them", we all thought.

We piled into their car finding it a bit of squash. I had to sit on Rob's lap as my sore ribs and broken arm couldn't cope with being squeezed between three others on the back seat. I don't remember it being a long journey, but I do remember the relief of finally arriving and looking forward to a good old cuppa and a rest. Crossing the threshold of their home the four of us were puzzled when we spied a large, roughly sawn hole in the ceiling at the top of the stairs with a wooden ladder propped up beneath it and what looked like the leg of a bed just visible inside. We politely asked if they'd had a leak.

"Oh, no, nothing like that" said Jen, "Our son sleeps up there, but don't worry he's not home at the moment."

Thinking this rather strange, we were keen to find out why their son wanted to sleep in the loft when they had perfectly serviceable bedroom space, but politeness stopped us from further enquiry. Jen then guided us up the stairs to a bedroom where Pete and Sue were to spend the night.

"Just need to make up the bed," she said as she rooted around in depths of the wash basket, dragging out a couple of sheets that had been mouldering away for a couple of weeks.

"Won't be a mo."

Sue and Pete watched in horror as Jen proceeded to make up the bed using the dirty linen chatting away cheerfully, totally oblivious to the looks of shock on our faces.

"I can't, I just can't sleep in that bed," whispered Sue to no one in particular once Jen was out of earshot.

With a sense of dread, Jen led us down the stairs to show Rob and me our accommodation for the night. Directed into the front room, it was our turn to be horrified as we were introduced to our sleeping arrangements; an old mattress on a litter-strewn floor, with just a ropey coverlet to keep us warm. We were all agog! I glanced at Rob, who was staring into the room in wide-eyed shock,

"Bloody hell, Jane," was all he could manage.

I felt sick.

"Jesus," I whispered. "You've gotta be joking!"

"OK, who wants a cuppa?" said Jen, not noticing how jittery we all were.

"No thanks," we all replied in unison having seen the state of the kitchen.

Not wanting to be rude after these people were good enough to put a roof over our heads, we said nothing further. We were dumbstruck anyway! What was this place! A squat? A drug den? It wasn't a restoration project as we had finally plucked up the courage to ask them the question, trying to make some sense of it all. Bill and Jen simply shrugged and muttered something about the house needing a bit of decorating. They were obviously masters of understatement.

Unfortunately for us, we had no choice but to stay, it being the dead of night and freezing cold outside. Sue and I were also tired, in pain and needed to rest.

As it turned out, resting was impossible. We all slept fitfully that night, jumping at every creak the house made, one eye open and focused on our luggage that we had moved near us for fear of it being stolen. We all remained fully clothed too, just in case we were attacked by rodents, crawled on by spiders, or needed to make a break for it.

The following morning, with all of us in need of a good shower or at the very least, a wash, Sue located the 'facilities' and was first into the bathroom. She exited remarkably quickly.

"You don't want to go in there!" she warned. "You REALLY don't. It's absolutely horrendous!"

She wasn't lying. We each entered in turn, gasped, did what we had to and retreated in ultra-quick time. Spending more than a couple of minutes was likely to result in a bad case of typhoid - I leave you to imagine the state of it. Though starving, breakfast was politely and unanimously refused after Bill blew a cloud of dust from the frying pan before throwing in a couple of rashers of bacon that he sniffed closely.

"Thought they'd be off. Been in the fridge for weeks! Remarkable how things keep these days," he said happily to four shocked adults trying hard not to vomit.

We never found out whether this couple owned the house or not and concluded they were a pair of eccentrics who seemed not to notice or care about the squalor surrounding them, most of it by their own hand. It was all very odd and we were anxious to get out of there. We finally escaped unharmed and Bill, still full of bonhomie, drove us to the car hire office. We thanked him for his 'hospitality' but avoided swapping addresses or phone numbers by quickly dashing into the premises before Bill had chance to ask.

"No way!" we all agreed.

Our scepticism regarding their French farmhouse purchase was now firmly justified.

Chapter 3
DECISIONS

A few years down the line from our strange encounter with Bill and Jen, our dream of buying a house in France was still refusing to go away. A close look at our finances revealed we could possibly afford to release some money from the equity in our UK home. By now, we had lived there for nearly two decades and mortgage interest rates had long ago dropped from the highs of 15%. At the same time, my salary had increased and Rob was now working for himself and doing well. The kids were happily settled and the Euro exchange rate was good. The realisation that the long held dream could finally become a reality hit home. I was beside myself but understood my excitable nature needed to be tempered somewhat. There was still a long way to go.

One dreary afternoon, I was on the computer again. I had been wasting time scanning a favourite website advertising French property for sale. I knew we still couldn't afford a lot and, after learning the lessons from others who had gone before us, had built a picture of what we *didn't* want:

(1) We hadn't the time to restore a wreck or try to make something habitable out of a smelly old pigsty.

(2) We didn't want something so remote it took an hour clomping across a muddy field to find our nearest neighbour or to locate a shop.

(3) We didn't want to buy land (cheap) and have a house built (not cheap).

(4) We didn't want a huge garden or several acres. Mowing grass, pulling weeds and ploughing the land were not our idea of a relaxing break. It being a holiday home, keeping a goat to keep the grass and weeds under control was out of the question too.

However, we were willing to redecorate and carry out DIY improvements, just as long as Rob dealt with any eight-legged residents first, and would be happy with any type of property that fell within our price range.

Other serious decisions we needed to make included exactly how much we could actually afford to spend. Did we want to be within driving distance of an airport, a port, the sea, lakes, mountains and/or cities? What about weather? Would we be happy in the north or would we prefer further south where we would find it warmer, necessitating a longer journey from the UK? My heart kept telling me the south east, but annoyingly my sensible head disagreed, reminding me we would get far more for our money elsewhere. That particular day, I'd pondered on a few properties in lovely areas, clicking on the interactive map and scrolling through the listings, but my mouse pointer kept sliding towards PACA (Provence Alpes Côte d'Azur), knowing full well, with our maximum price in place, nothing wonderful was going to show up.

It had been easy to fall in love this varied and stunning region after spending many a happy holiday there. Covering some 12,100 square miles, it is comprised of six Departments:

Var, Vaucluse, Alpes Maritimes, Alpes de Haute Provence and the Haute Alpes, and bordered by Italy in the east, the Mediterranean in the south, Occitanie in the west, and the Auvergne-Rhône Alpes in the north. You have the Mediterranean to play in, mountains to ski or hike in, lakes to swim or fish in and hundreds of amazing villages to lodge in. There are cities to shop in and airports to fly into. With, on average, 300 days of sunshine a year, it also has perfect weather. What's not to like? Well, with much of it classified as the most expensive in which to buy, own and maintain property in all of France, after Paris, we recognised early on that it was simply out of reach. Wistfully, clicking away on the mouse button that day, I actually stopped breathing for a second or two when the Web produced a list of properties for sale and some were within our price range. Crikey! Was this for real?

On closer examination, most were still beyond our meagre means, but scanning further, I came across a four-bedroom apartment in the Alpes de Haute Provence. From the description given, it sounded just perfect for us. The apartment was in a small wood-clad building of four apartments, standing on the banks of a little trout lake. Inside it seemed huge and included a library and a mezzanine. It was also on sale at a surprisingly low price. With the exchange rate still markedly in our favour, it seemed an absolute bargain and almost too good to be true. On the page was a link to the *Immobilier* selling the apartment. My finger paused over the mouse button. I briefly held a 'should I, shouldn't I' argument with myself. A couple of minutes later, after giving in to my impulsive nature, I clicked on the link, completed the online enquiry form and sent it off. Almost immediately, I got cold feet, but what had now been done could not be undone. I told myself I hadn't signed anything and I would probably not hear back from the agent because the place was most likely sold already. I decided not to worry and kept my little secret carefully tucked away. No need to bother Rob with it yet.

The next morning, Mrs Impulsive returned, shortly after I received a response from the agent explaining the apartment was still for sale and when would we like to view it. As a full-time college lecturer and it being September, my next holiday was the half-term break in October. Off went my email and the date was set.

Now to tackle Rob…

To Rob: "I've done something. It's to do with France."

It was in late September when I let Rob into my naughty little secret, all the while hoping he wouldn't get mad with me. He didn't. He was probably relieved I wasn't confessing to adultery or more seriously, being the cause of major bodywork repairs to the car. In fact, he greeted my happy admission quite calmly, which is very normal for him. He doesn't get over-excited at the prospect of a holiday, a live concert or trips to the cinema to see a film he has wanted to see for ages.Neither does he go overboard because it is his birthday or Christmas Day. He keeps telling me he is happy and excited about such events, but doesn't need to scream, jump about and generally go nuts, which is the way I usually react. I tell him it is because he's a Pisces, all calm waters, and I'm a Leo, fiery with a tendency to love the limelight and in this case, I had been buzzing to tell him about the appointment I'd made to see a property in the Alpes de Haute Provence.

Chapter 4
FINDING THE DREAM PROPERTY

In the run-up to our trip to France, we found ourselves excited, but chewing our fingernails with worry and stress. The excitement is obviously explained, but the worry? Well, this was new territory for us, a trip into the unknown. I might have done enough research to write an encyclopaedia on the subject, but actually 'doing' it was nerve-racking; this was for real. How could we go through this enormous purchase and part with loads of hard-earned dosh when we didn't speak much French? What if the *Immobilier* is a crook? He could rip us off. Where is the upper Verdon Valley anyway? Are there any shops? How do we get there? What about furniture? We mulled all this over, and a whole lot more throughout the weeks leading up to the visit, finally getting a grip on our nerves and managing to regrow our fingernails. We dealt with the language question by roping in our old school mate, Bob, who having married his French sweetheart, had been living near Lyon for over 25 years. We had lost contact with him not long after leaving school, but *Friends Reunited* had united us once more. Since reconnecting, we had stayed with Bob and Sylviane at their home on several occasions and they often stayed with us for a night when visiting family in the Midlands. Sylviane was fluent in English and Bob was fluent in French, and what we desperately needed now were their translating skills.

Feeling a lot more confident knowing the *Immobilier* hadn't a hope of pulling the wool over our eyes as Bob and Sylviane agreed to accompany us, we left for France at the start of the half-term holiday, driving our old Range Rover, a rather flattering shade of sludge green, which Rob had bought for a song. We were to find out exactly why, but more of that later.

We stayed with Bob and Sylviane for the night and awoke to the smell of freshly brewed coffee and busy sounds emanating from the kitchen. Forever the early bird, Sylviane was already preparing breakfast before our brains had registered the sun was shining and it was time to get up. Leaving their home an hour later, we emerged into a perfect autumn morning. Frost had formed overnight, sprinkled on grassy banks and fallen leaves like decoration on a cake, lending the air a wonderful freshness that coloured our cheeks a healthy pink and turned our warm breath to vapour. Mother nature had smiled and granted us the perfect weather for our journey.

Our route took us through stunning mountain scenery beyond Grenoble where we joined the route Napoleon for a time. As it wended its way towards Nice and its beaches, a swim in the Mediterranean was far from our minds as we turned off at a small village and headed towards the mountains. Shortly afterwards, we arrived at our destination and booked into a small hotel for the night. With bags dumped in rooms, it was time to head off and meet Antoine.

Antoine was the *Immobilier* and Antoine was the absolute cliché of a Frenchman who spoke English; if you've ever seen an English chap perform an exaggerated impression of a French chap speaking English (like Peter Sellers as Inspector Clouseau in *The Pink Panther*) you'll understand what I mean. I was fascinated! He was relatively young, probably in his thirties, knew his stuff and was surprisingly exuberant. After all the *bonjours* were out of the way and introductions made, Antoine launched into his sales pitch, or more correctly, a reverse sales pitch. In France, the *Immobilier* works for the buyer, not the seller. We found this out the minute he started speaking.

"You 'ave come to see zis apartement non?" showing us the image from the advertisement.

"Oui" we muttered, feeling a little nervous.

"You will not like zis. Eet is 'orrible. Eet 'as bad insides," he said as he was throwing his arms up in the air for effect.

"Pardon?" We both said in unison, wondering if we had heard him correctly.

Ignoring us and without drawing breath he continued, *"Eet was louer for many many times and zeez people, zey not look after eet. Zer are plugs, zey 'ang out of ze walls but, je ne sais pas, p'raps you like to, 'ow you say ... ah, restore,"* he said with an exaggerated shrug of the shoulders. *"You go see eet an' then you tell me. I sink you no like eet"*, he finished, giving us a sympathetic frown accompanied by another shrug of the shoulders.

With mouths hanging open, we tried in vain to say something sensible, but simply stood gawping at him while he regarded us with a bemused look. He then thrust two photos at us and pointing to each in turn, he explained:

"Zis one is a petite 'ouse. Eet is very good. In bon état, Très joli. You go see eet aussi," he ordered.

"Ze second is an autre apartement. Zis is nouveau, new. Eet is good aussi," nodding with pleasure to have found another two properties in case we were disappointed with the first.

We thanked him politely and smiled as he called over a young woman whom he introduced as Michelle, his assistant.

"She is taking you for ze viewing. You use your car, oui? She speak good Engleesh." He then slid a small form across the desk towards us. *"S'il vous plaît, you sign 'ere,"* he said pointing to the appropriate place.

Puzzled, we peered at the document wondering whether we were about to sign our lives away before viewing anything but Bob and Sylviane calmed our nerves by explaining that signing meant we were agreeing for Antoine to temporarily remove the properties from sale, therefore allowing no other viewing until we had made any decisions concerning them. It was a way of preventing 'gazumping'. If we chose to buy, at whatever price we agreed with the seller, this was set and no one could outbid us, even during the 'cooling off' period. Those properties rejected would then be reinstated 'for sale'.

As we were ushered out of the door, Rob and I wondered if the apartment was as bad as Antoine described.

"He'd have been great in *'Allo 'Allo,*" Rob said as we climbed into the car.

Property One

Michelle proved to be an excellent guide, speaking English like a native. She explained her mum was English and her Dad was Dutch, she was fluent in both, as well as French and Italian. As we drove through the most amazing scenery on this bright sunny day towards our first property, she provided a lot of insight into life in the valley. She pointed out the names of the little villages along the way, answered our questions and enquired as to what it was that made us want to buy in France. Our journey passed quickly and in no time we arrived at our first viewing, the apartment that Antoine had verbally demolished.

Michelle directed us into a large car park where we could see, gathered on the edge of the small lake, a cluster of wood-clad buildings. The autumn sun continued to shine and felt warm on our backs as we made our way over a small wooden bridge that led us past a restaurant and into a central area. At this point, Rob and I were completely dazzled by the beauty of the surroundings and were praying that Antoine's derisory description of the property was over the top. Once inside the apartment we knew he had been right, the plugs **were** hanging out of the walls with exposed wiring everywhere. Ceilings were collapsing and the whole structure looked unsafe. It was in a terrible state. Stepping outside onto a tiny balcony, we could see the exterior was almost as run down as the interior. Bob, who was a joiner by trade, was shaking his head advising us it would take a lot of money to put right. We were profoundly disappointed as we had been looking forward to this for months. This simply wasn't the French property we had always dreamed of.

As we crossed the little bridge, heading back to the car with heavy hearts, Rob turned to me and said we wouldn't have wanted it anyway.

"Why not?" I asked.

"Mozzies," he said.

"Eh? What are you going on about?"

"Mozzies ... in the summer. That lake is still water. It's a breeding ground for them."

At this point, I should state that mosquitos see Rob as a 3-star Michelin meal. They just love him – the poor soul is bitten a lot and often has a bad reaction to the bites. One bite on the wrist has caused the whole of his forearm to swell. When not suffering this extreme reaction, he still scratches the bites non-stop, thereby causing a myriad of scabs resembling a bad case of chicken pox. Of course, he is my ideal deterrent as the little sods fly past me and head straight for him instead. He has used every lotion and spray known to man to thwart the mozzie's efforts, but apart from making him smell as if he's bathed in the stuff for months at a time, they still find him delicious.

"Do they have mosquitos in the mountains?" I asked.

"Those nasty bastards will live anywhere," said Rob, giving me a wry grin.

With disappointment still weighing heavily upon us, this was Rob's way of making me smile. He has a knack of making me laugh at the most stupid of things. I gave him a playful punch on the arm and climbed into the car feeling a little better.

Property Two

We set off to view the next property; the little house that Antoine had selected for us. It was ten minutes further away along the valley and positioned just outside a pretty, old walled village. After climbing a steep and very narrow road that twisted its way up the mountainside, Michelle directed us onto an unpaved track and told us to stop. Once out of the car, we stood and just gazed at the view. It was stunning. I don't think anyone moved, except Michelle who had entered the house and was busily engaged in opening the doors and all the shutters. We were in awe, surrounded by mountains, their peaks bathed in sunshine. The air was so fresh we filled our lungs and just marvelled as we looked down the valley from our vantage point. It was quiet, so quiet that we could hear the youthful river Verdon as it gushed its way down the valley. The trees, which filled the mountainsides, dazzled in their autumn colours and the soothing sound of a cowbell emanated from a herd of white cattle grazing in the field below us. In the distance, nestled in the valley by a bend in the road, you could just see the top of a little fort. I thought we had landed in heaven.

A shout from the doorway of the house brought our attention back to the business in hand and we headed indoors. Rob, Bob and Sylviane had hurried after Michelle as she moved about showing them the interior, I was lagging behind because I had stopped dead to take it all in. This little house was perfect in every way: the oak beam over the large log-burning fireplace, the wood-clad walls exactly right for a home in the mountains, the modern American-style kitchen and the lovely wooden spiral staircase that led to the three bedrooms.

Shaking myself out of this attack of reverie, I eventually made it upstairs to mooch around. The largest of the bedrooms had walls covered in fabric placed over padding of some sort. Whoever did it was extremely skilled in needlework, but sadly lacking in design flair as the pattern was so busy it made your head ache; think miniature patchwork and quilted anorak on all four walls, even the curtains. It was like a nightmarish padded cell. As awful as it was, I knew any decorating issues could easily be sorted in time and thankfully, the remaining two rooms had the same décor as the ground floor, with just some minor sprucing up required. Each bedroom had a low window and gazing through them in turn, the breathtaking views continued to inspire wonder and I imagined the joy of waking up to such vistas each morning.

Back downstairs, I stepped out onto the balcony that ran the full width of the house, mesmerised by that view. After a couple of minutes, Sylviane came to join me saying,

"This is perfect Jane; it is just so beautiful here".

When Rob arrived and stood alongside us, I was finding it hard to contain my excitement.

"We've just got to buy this! The view, the house ... it's just amazing! Perfect! I gushed. "It's everything we've always wanted."

He looked at me and in his own inimitable calm way, sagely said, "It is great, but let's not jump the gun, we've got the third property to see first which we might like even better. You never know. Then we can make a proper decision."

Property Three and an Easy Decision

It was very difficult dragging ourselves away, but Michelle was on a mission and needed us to see the final property. It was situated in a much larger village further up the valley, located above a supermarket. There was nothing wrong with the apartment, but it wasn't for us. It was modern and fairly roomy with rear patio doors opening onto a huge terrace the size of a football pitch. The problem was the terrace faced north and the sun's rays would slowly creep away around the side of the building and beyond, leaving it in shade for most of the day. From my point of view, nothing would match up to the little house and Rob now knew it too. It just had to be ours.

Back at the *Immobilier*, Antoine was awaiting our return.

"*You like any of zeez properties?*" he questioned, with a look that indicated he might have guessed already.

We told him we loved the little house, that the apartment in the large village was ok, and that the first apartment was exactly, if not worse, than he described.

"*Ha! I knew you will not like eet! So, you want to buy zee 'ouse, oui?*"

"Yes, we'd love to" said Rob as I did an excited dance next to him.

Antoine smiled. "*Excellent! I will ring ze owners now. You will not pay ze price zay ask. I will make offer for you,*" he stated while picking up the phone.

After a few minutes, Antoine had pushed for a lower price with the current owners and we agreed immediately to go ahead with the purchase. We left his office walking on air, not quite believing we were soon to become the owners of a French house. Bob and Sylviane were thrilled for us. That night we all celebrated with some good wine and a great meal at our hotel. We had finally done it. That gorgeous little house was going to be ours.

After breakfast the next morning, before heading north to deliver Bob and Sylviane back to their home, we decided to return to the little house for another look. It was a lovely morning, bright and fresh, but the watery sun began to play a game of hide and seek, scuttling behind clouds and emerging for brief moments only to disappear for good as the morning progressed. Although the warmth had fled along with the sunshine, the rain was held at bay and wrapping up warmly, we headed off for another viewing, fully aware we were unable to access to the interior of the house. It wasn't a problem. We were happy enough knowing it was ours. Instead, we spent the time drinking in the spectacular surroundings and wandering around the commune, making plans and wondering if our French neighbours would approve of us when the time came for us to move in.

Finally dragging ourselves away, we took a quick trip to the larger village further along the valley intending to take a different route back home over the Col, the highest point on the road, heading towards Gap and Grenoble. It was then that our Range Rover decided to show its true colours by juddering, coughing and spluttering into the village before dying completely next to a bus stop. Great. As is the tendency with most men, Bob and Rob climbed out of the car, poked about under the bonnet for a few minutes and then had a very serious discussion, looking like a couple of forensic pathologists poring over a crime scene.

"What's wrong with it?" we girls wanted to know.

"Dunno. We can't see anything obvious. Let's give it another go," said Rob as Bob stood peering at the engine while Rob was trying to start it. Unfortunately, there was no hope of resuscitation this time. We had one dead Rangie.

Following a panicky phone call, our insurance company arranged with a garage to come and collect our deceased vehicle. We hung around the bus stop, waving away any buses who thought we wanted to get on. We had no idea when the *dépannage* (breakdown) truck would arrive and therefore couldn't wander off in search of sustenance. Hungry, thirsty and bored witless, we did a happy jig when, after several hours, the truck finally crested the brow of the hill and pulled up.

Bob handled the conversation, conducted in rapid fire French, while the rest of us hung around sporting gloomy expressions, worrying about work commitments.

"What's he say?" said Rob

"The car is being taken to Gap," Bob explained.

"What? That's bloody miles away!"

Their conversation was temporarily interrupted when the driver, having loaded our Rangie onto the trailer, delivered a round of oily handshakes and gave cheery *'Au revoir'* before getting into his cab and driving off.

Oh, what joy, we thought as we waved car and truck off and were left stranded. A taxi eventually took us back to the hotel we'd checked out of earlier. The receptionist was surprised to see us again, so we outlined our problem. *"Quelquefois, zees sings 'appen"* he said with that Gallic pout and shrug of the shoulders.

Next morning, the autumn sun had emerged from its hiding place and a hard frost had settled in the valley, coating everything in a shimmering silver glaze. After munching on bread and jam and several croissants each while downing several cups of milky coffee, we took a short walk in the frigid air in an attempt to digest our excess carbohydrate and to blow away some of those early morning cobwebs that infest the mind. Feeling refreshed, it wasn't long before we were in a taxi heading for Gap to pick up the Rangie. The drive was going to take more than two hours and the roads proved to be narrow, steep and full of hairpin bends. Our taxi driver obviously had yearnings to be an international rally driver, but without the training, or the car. He got us there faster than delivery by helicopter. After the most hair-raising journey, we fell out of the taxi, relieved to have finally arrived without throwing up any undigested breakfast or suffering serious injury. The Rangie was thankfully ready to go after having had a replacement rubber hose for an oil cooler fitted. The garage had not been in possession of the actual part, the owner told us, and it would take several days for it to arrive if ordered in. Luckily for us, he owned a Range Rover and offered to replace the part for free, using the one from his own, knowing we needed it urgently to continue our journey home and return to work. I wasn't prepared to face the wrath of my fellow lecturers who, after a week off, would return to the stress of having to cover my classes in addition to their own. Sylviane was also dreading the response of her manager if she didn't turn up to work as expected.

We have often been caught out by the kindness shown to us by the French we have met, destroying the myth that 'the French don't like us', usually followed by, 'and we don't like them either'. Total rubbish of course, stated by Brits who have never set foot in the country, or who have spent a few days in Paris, no doubt demanding everything in English and expecting understanding.

On our journey back home, after saying goodbye to our

lovely friends and thanking them for their assistance, we finally telephoned the kids and told them about the house we had bought. They were full of questions, but we said we would fill them in when we got back. Fortunately, before leaving the UK, we had borrowed my father-in-law's video camera. We thought it wise to film the properties so we would have a record of them when we got home. In the cold light of day, we could visit again, showing the family too, confirming that our decision had been the right one.

It was!

Chapter 5
PLANNING AND PREPPING

Within a week of returning home, a large brown envelope plopped onto the mat by the front door. It was all the required paperwork concerning our purchase. Thankfully, the majority of the *Compromis de Vente* had been translated into English. For those of you who might not know, this is the legal and binding contract between the purchaser and the buyer and we needed to complete a lot of detailed information. Most of this was normal stuff: dates of birth, full names, address, etc., but we thought it a tad weird when we had to supply the name of the church in which we were married and the name of the vicar who married us! We pondered on what people would be required to do if they were married in other venues, say a sandy beach under a palm tree in the Caribbean perhaps or a wedding in Vegas, the service conducted by an Elvis Presley lookalike singing the Hawaiian Wedding song!

It took a while to get the job done as we often had to ferret around in family or household documents just to be sure we'd got the facts right. Finally, after a day or two, we were able to return the paperwork to Antoine. Keeping a copy for reference, it meant we now had the seller information, their names and address and the name and address of the *Notaire* who would work on behalf of us all. We also knew we had a ten-day cooling off period in case we wanted to withdraw, which was about as likely as Rob liking mosquitos.

We'd already had 'the chat' with our bank who was happy to let us proceed and the deposit was duly processed and sent. The date for signing the *Acte de Vente* at the *Notaire*'s office was set for January and we were to move into our little house during my February half-term break.

With Christmas and New Year out of the way, we began to make plans: flights to get us there for the official signing and the ferry for the half term. I also needed to scrounge a day off work. We drew up a list of everything we needed to furnish and equip the house and began to shop for the smaller items. It was like setting up home for the first time, though a lot of what we had in our very first home had been donated by parents or bought second-hand from the small ads in the local paper.

I will never forget the little rented flat that was our first home together, in a private block with an unparalleled vista overlooking the British Leyland plant where Rob was working as an apprentice. Occasionally, with the wind in the right direction, the scent of the coolant used on the hot cutting tools wafted in through an open window, but we didn't care one jot, we were young, it was ours and we loved it, for a while anyway. This was the 70s, a time when we were to be found decked out in platform-soled shoes and loud clothing. The flat was no different as, when it came to the decorating, we avidly pursued the most lurid of colour schemes. We thought it looked cool. I have vivid memories of the ultra-bright, ultra-patterned orange and brown wallpaper we hung in the hallway, and the purple we had on the walls, the bedding and carpet in the bedroom!

I remember we stretched to buying the washing machine, a fridge, a revolting nylon living room carpet in brown and our bed. We had saved for over 12 months while living with my parents to acquire these possessions, but everything else were cast offs. Our baby daughter was sleeping in one half of a set of bunk beds, which, along with some bright yellow curtains, were donated by my in-laws, her bedroom carpet came from a friend, bedding, towels and odds and sods for the kitchen were wedding presents, and my mum and dad bought us a new dining set.

My parents were also eager to dispose of their old sofa and chairs, no doubt needing to get something comfortable instead, so donated the old ones to us. The design of this suite was very popular at the time, consisting of gold nylon cushion covers, which, when sat upon, created so much static your hair would stand on end, enhanced by the static from the nylon carpet. The black vinyl covering also made you sweat if you lingered too long. It did us for a couple of years, but we couldn't wait to get rid of it. A small mouse, which had taken up residence, helped it on its way when said mouse chewed out the bottom of the sofa and made a comfortable home inside. We and the mouse moved out into separate dwellings and we dumped the suite in the process.

Moving into the French house was the only other time we had to furnish an entire property from scratch. In other house moves, as with most people, furniture and household stuff moved with us. This made shopping for our French abode exciting and even Rob, who usually hates trailing around the shops, agreed to tag along sometimes, enjoying his occasional forays. Largely though, he left it to me, saying I was better at it, the usual phrase he uses when he doesn't want to do something. I, however, was in my element.

As the household goods started to pile up, we stored them in a bedroom at home. Rob concentrated on trying to source a trailer large enough to take everything and ensuring the Range Rover could cope with dragging it along mountain roads.

The evening before our departure to France and the *Notaire*'s office, it started to snow. We watched forlornly from the window as huge flakes sailed past and started to build a hefty layer. Normally, we would be beside ourselves with excitement as, being skiers, we both love the snow and get childishly silly if we are lucky to get any in the Midlands. This time, however, we were worrying about our flight. We were due out of Luton at some God-awful hour having sourced cheap tickets. We would have preferred to fly out of Birmingham at a reasonable time, but as we didn't register anywhere on the rich list this proved impossible. We checked the weather reports for Luton, expecting to see cancellations, but it seemed the snow had missed that part of the country entirely. Crunching up the drive at just past midnight, we set off, knowing we would become official owners of our property the following day. Or so we thought!

After a long trip, most of it requiring careful driving through a blizzard, we finally found ourselves crossing the line between snow and no snow. We had booked our flight with a well-known budget airline that will remain nameless for reasons that will become clear.

In the terminal, we joined the long queue taking a hideously long time reaching the desk. Once within earshot, it seemed many passengers had been refused boarding due to an untold problem. This problem revealed itself when we were finally faced with two check-in desk employees who looked about 15 years old. The conversation went something like this:

Check-in One, looking peed off: "Yeah? Can I help?"

Us: "Yes please, we're booked on the flight to Nice this morning," smiling politely.

Check-in One: "Names?"

We happily gave our names and had passports ready.

Check-in One: "Sorry, the flight has been cancelled."

Us: "What! Why?"

Check-in One, shrugging: "Don't know."

Turning to Check-in Two: "Do you know why the Nice flight has been cancelled?"

Check-in Two, sounding bored: "They've lost the plane … don't know where it's gone."

Us, surprised and puzzled: What!" "What do you mean? How can you lose a plane?"

Check-in Two: It's been sent somewhere else but we don't know where."

After a moment's silence with no further comment from the teenagers, other than a look implying the conversation was over and we should move along, we persisted. We were not happy that after four hours on the road, we had received this news from two youngsters with attitude and no offer of help or any alternative.

Us, a little put out: "Look, we've GOT to get to Nice. We have a very important solicitor's appointment. Please, have you a flight that leaves later this morning that we can take instead?"

Check-in One, after clicking on her computer and giving us a blank look: "No, it's full."

Us, sounding desperate: What about tomorrow morning?"

Check-in One: More clicking on the computer: "No, it's full."

The whole situation then began to turn into a bit of a farce. One after the other we named alternatives, shamelessly begging for all we were worth. Could we go from Stanstead or Gatwick, Heathrow or even Bristol? What about ANY airport near enough for us to drive to that day or the following day? Each time, our check-in girl clicked on her computer keyboard and said, "No, it's full", fixing us with a bored expression. She had obviously used the *'computer sez no'* sketch from *Little Britain* as her training video.

We were getting nowhere fast. To obtain a refund on our flights and car hire, we were reluctantly directed towards another queue. It was another long wait before being told we would have to claim online. It took the company three months to pay us back. We also lost the money on the car hire.

"Never again!" we said, "We will NEVER, EVER book with that useless airline again!"

Thankfully, things have improved since then and we are aware that with the advent of new regulations for flight companies, our shoddy treatment back then would, in today's world, have consequences, but we still haven't risked it.

Feeling gloomy and frustrated, we headed back to the car to think about what our next move could be. We first checked scheduled flights out of Birmingham, but it seemed only first-class seats were available. No wonder when they told us the price of the tickets! Our only alternative was to drive down and delay our *Notaire's* appointment until the following day.

We booked Eurotunnel. The snow had hit the extreme southeast badly and we knew we would have to take the long way around to get there, but we would have done anything. We urgently needed to complete the buying process. We couldn't get over again before our planned 'moving in' week during February half term and we couldn't move in unless we owned the house.

As it was, and in marked contrast to the treatment we had received from the sullen airline staff, we were struck by the kindness of those involved in our purchase who came to our rescue. We had started the ball rolling by making a call to Sylviane, asking if she would telephone Antoine to explain the situation. For us, speaking French over the telephone was and still is nerve-racking. We didn't think we would have much success in trying to understand Antoine's mashed English either. Better to leave it to a French native we thought.

Job done, Sylviane rang us back to say that Antoine was contacting the sellers, letting them know about our cancelled flights and our new arrangements. About ten minutes later, we received a further call from Sylviane. Antoine had got back to her and explained that Michel and Sylvanna, the sellers, had said we were not to panic, we could move in as planned. They would leave the keys for us to find on arrival in February and we could carry out the official signing at some point during that week. Michel was concerned that we should not have to face the long journey that day, forced to cope with the difficult driving conditions in northern France where there had also been a heavy snowfall. Antoine had also stressed we were not to worry about our appointment as he would ring the *Notaire* to agree a new one and would confirm the day and time by email. After cancelling the tunnel and feeling huge relief and gratitude, we left Luton behind and headed back home.

Chapter 6
MOVING IN AT LAST

During the final couple of weeks before my February half-term break and hopefully facing a problem-free journey to France, we sourced the larger pieces of furniture. We had a plan of the interior of the French house and knew what would fit. Without too much searching, we found comfy sofas and dining furniture which were the perfect size. We also located the bedroom furniture, which had to be flat pack, as we knew there was no way we could manoeuvre a fully constructed bed up the narrow spiral staircase. The store then kindly agreed to hang onto it all until we'd picked up the trailer that Rob had rented, which closely resembled a horsebox, though I'm sure any horses would have objected strongly due to the absence of any windows. To avoid the dangers of acquiring hernias or pulled muscles, the furniture was loaded with assistance from the store's forklift truck and its driver. How we were going to unload it all at the other end never entered our heads.

Finally, the day before leaving, Rob and his brother got to grips with packing the trailer to the roof with all the paraphernalia we had stored in the bedroom. They were very studious about it. One of them would emerge from the trailer, give it a careful examination and shout instructions to the other who would be inside moving stuff about. The purpose of this scrutiny was to ensure it was packed properly, distributing the weight evenly, thereby avoiding the appearance of it containing a Shetland pony on one side and a carthorse on the other.

Door to door, the journey to our French house is one thousand miles. Rob's brother and wife agreed to accompany us to help with the moving in process. Rob and his brother, Tez, come as a double act. They are very close to one another in affection, age and humour. As youngsters, they'd seemingly spent most of their time getting up to no good, stories of which they've dined out on many a time over the years; their audience reduced to tear-inducing hysterics. Their parents were oblivious to it all. They were too busy looking after the additional six siblings. As the four of us have spent many a happy holiday under canvas, with our respective children, Tez and Jan were the natural choice to travel with us.

The plan for this journey was for Rob or Tez to do most of the driving and for me to help if necessary. For some reason, we thought it a great idea to travel overnight and complete the journey in one hit. This meant catching a ferry at what we called 'stupid o'clock'. Approaching Dover, our stress levels temporarily shot up when a knocking noise emanated from the front end of the Rangie. We pulled over and the boys, both with puzzled expressions, conducted their examination of the engine and the wheels, pushing on the tyres and peering underneath to see if something was about to come loose. After a short discussion, they climbed back in saying that everything appeared ok. The Rangie, it seemed, was joking as the noise magically disappeared.

We had an uneventful journey, punctuated with occasional stops to grab a coffee or to take a comfort break. It was during one of these stops that Janice, in desperate need of a loo break, hurried off to do what she had to. After several minutes, we spied her, running like something demented back to the car. Jumping in and breathing heavily with the effort, obviously in a panic, she slammed the door and sunk low into her seat.

"Drive, drive!" She gasped.

"Why"? We asked.

"Just drive will you!" she demanded. "I need to get away. NOW!"

"You committed a robbery then, Jan?" Joked Tez.

"No, don't be stupid! Please can we just go? I don't want to be seen," she pleaded.

This was very, very unusual behaviour for Janice. She doesn't move quickly, unless there is a flying insect within ten feet of her. Then she turns into a complete maniac, arms flailing, mouth screaming, desperate to get away. Much to the amusement of fellow drinkers, she once cleared an entire table of beverages in a pub beer garden when a wasp appeared, looking for something tasty to munch on. The wasp escaped unharmed and Janice, who is normally quite shy and incapable of doing anything untoward, was left very red-faced.

On this occasion, while suffering a bout of IBS, she had arrived at the services and rushed to the toilet, the hole in the ground variety, (which we have always nicknamed a 'stand and deliver') and wasn't quite in position when nature powerfully took its course. She was mortified and desperate to get away before being identified as the guilty party. I suffer with the same condition and know what it feels like to endure such indignities and embarrassment, so I did have some sympathy, but her reaction was so out of character and such a hoot that it has gone down in family history!

Later, we realised we might have been rather misguided doing the 'overnight' thing. After no sleep the night before and a drive of nine hours, we were finally feeling the effects, weariness creeping over us like a blanket. Our theory of achieving our destination in one go had crashed and burned, so that night we booked into a hotel along the route, situated just south of Grenoble. We climbed out of the car into the darkness, stretching out our cramped limbs as we did so. It had been snowing, that 'proper' snow that creaks and crunches under foot. It was freezing cold, but beautiful. The sky was clear and full of stars. We stood for a while looking heavenwards, trying to identify the constellations and gazed at the mountains silhouetted against the night sky. Before heading into the warmth of the hotel, the contents of the trailer were checked to ensure they hadn't been thrown into chaos after our journey and we offered our thanks to the Rangie for behaving.

It was quite a large hotel and we were the only guests. Initially it felt a little creepy, as if we had walked into the hotel from the Shining but without Jack Nicholson and his manic smile. Thankfully, we were not about to be murdered by an axe-wielding lunatic as we were welcomed warmly by our hosts, even though we had arrived late. They were obviously happy to see paying guests and ignored the fact we were clomping about shaking snow from our boots all over the reception floor. After checking in, we were escorted up the staircase, leaving the melting snow and puddles behind, and shown to our rooms; clean, warm and snuggly. I think we were ready to collapse there and then, but rumblings from our empty stomachs were a reminder we needed to eat. After a hot meal and a few glasses of wine, we slept like babies.

The next morning, breakfasted and thoroughly refreshed, we headed off. Only three hours to go. Once again, the Rangie scuppered our plans. An hour or two into the journey, happily trundling along, we rounded a bend when an almighty bump came from underneath the car. Rob slowed and pulled over. Jan and I watched from the backseat as the boys got out, walked around the car and back along the road a short distance, returning with a large lump of metal.

"What's that?" we said.

"It's the prop shaft," they said.

"What's one of those?" we asked.

"Means we've lost four wheel drive," they answered.

"Oh, God! Does that mean we can't get to the house?" we asked in a panic.

"Nah, it'll be fine, we'll get there ok," they lied.

I could almost imagine the Rangie laughing at us.

Janice and I had no idea what a prop shaft did but were extremely happy to know that we could continue with our journey. The boys looked serious, knowing we might have problems in store. We finally grasped why they had been so worried when the Rangie, obviously feeling guilty, managed to get us at least half way up the snowy road towards the house before stopping like a stubborn horse refusing a jump. With the weight of the trailer, the steepness of the slope, the snowy surface and with only two-wheel drive, we hadn't a hope. We then started to slide backwards. Holding our collective breath and gripping on for dear life, we almost cheered when Rob managed to prevent our certain death by stopping the slide before we plunged over the edge.

"OMG! I thought we were going to die," said Janice, voice trembling. "My stomach is doing summersaults!"

"I hope we're not going to get a repeat of the services saga," said Tez.

"Well, she'll have to go behind that tree over there," said Rob pointing, trying not to laugh.

"And wipe your bum using snow," I said, giggling.

"Oh, very funny," Janice responded. "You're not going to let me get over that motorway services incident are you?"

"No, way!" was our joint response.

At that moment, a Mitsubishi Shogan drew up behind us and out stepped Michel, the previous owner of our little house. We thought we might be hallucinating. He was never forewarned of our imminent arrival, and whether it was all our stars aligning or Michel having psychic powers, I don't know, but we were mightily thrilled to see him, **and** his vehicle, which was equipped with a tow bar.

Michel explained he was returning to his new holiday home following a trip to the village, informing us he and Sylvanna were staying for a few days to attend the *Notaire's* meeting later that week. Michel proved to be a real superstar. After allowing us to move in before we officially owned the place, he then saved our bacon by towing the trailer to the house for us. He was incredibly helpful in demonstrating how things worked, informing us about the annual *copropriété* meeting we had to attend, plus a whole host of interesting and important matters. He left us, after delivering the bad news that EDF would not be out until Monday, two days away, to restore full power to the house and that until then, we'd hardly any electricity to play with. He wished us '*Bonne chance!*'

It was freezing inside, requiring several layers of clothing, gloves and hats in an attempt to ward off frostbite. We could switch the heating on in one room, but this meant no lights or the ability to boil a kettle. We could switch on one light and boil the kettle but no heat. We certainly could not warm up the huge water tank that resided under the house, even with everything switched off. So, no showers. We had to prioritise.

While we still had daylight, we started to unload the essentials. The sofas were deemed vital and awarded priority status. Standing around in the snow, eyeing these large and very heavy objects we lamented the fact that commonsense had fled on the day they were loaded. As Rob and Tez lacked the physique and strength of *Superman*, it was going to prove a bit of a problem getting them inside.

"This is ridiculous. How the hell are we going to manoeuvre the things down those steps, through two narrow doorways and around that blasted 90-degree turn" groaned Rob.

"Dunno" said Tez. "Don't think the forklift truck fairy will turn up any time soon and grant us a wish either. Got no choice bro. C'mon, we'd better get on with it before we die of exposure."

Dragging the first out of the trailor, they managed to lift it a few inches off the ground, edging it along, bit by tiny bit, stopping every couple of seconds to put it down to avoid passing out with the effort. It wasn't long before arguments broke out and the air was turning blue.

"Bloody hell Rob, hang on to it! Can't you lift it more your end?"

"I am! It's all right for you; I'm bearing most of the weight, stop pushing for God's sake!"

"Who's pushing ... I'm NOT pushing!" Tez yelled.

After manipulating it down the steps, the arguments continued as they negotiated the first doorway.

"Turn it to your left ... NO ... **Your** Left ... L E F T!" Tez spelled out through gritted teeth due to the effort of holding the sofa off the ground.

"I am, you idiot ... Shit! It won't fit. Put it down, PUT IT DOWN! I'm going to drop the damn thing!" said Rob as he felt the sofa sliding out of his grip.

"OK OK, keep yer hair on!" Tez responded.

This went on until both sofas were finally in place. The

relief was tangible, but the moaning about aching muscles and how one or the other of them escaped near death by heart attack, or avoided being flattened by a dropped sofa, went on for quite a while. At least the seating was sorted and the brothers survived the ordeal.

The remainder of the household furniture, much of it flat pack, would require a lot less sweaty endeavour and accompanying expletives, except for three double mattresses that proved a little more problematic. It was all very *Laurel and Hardy* with Rob and Tez literally fighting the first one, struggling to force it up the spiral staircase. The mattress often won the fight as Rob pulled and Tez pushed, attempting to fold it in half to get it around the curve. The mattress had other ideas and simply sprung back again. Watching this game of push me, pull you, Jan and I were in hysterics. Red-faced and after more swearing, the boys eventually won the battle. Pity I hadn't that video camera. We might have been better off by £250 after submitting this comedy of errors to *You've Been Framed*!

That evening, with most of the essentials in place, the remainder could wait until the following day. Thanks to the hob running from the gas bottle stored under the house, refreshments had been prepped and consumed. Happily basking in the heat from the log fire, enjoying its soporific effect, we were reluctant to leave its comforting warmth to venture upstairs to bed. Braving the chilly bedrooms and the freezing bedding, we eventually managed to drag ourselves away when eyelids grew heavy and Rob had started to snore!

The following day was spent constructing the flat-pack bedroom furniture and emptying the trailer, carefully stowing items in the appropriate place. By the end of the day, happily snuggled in front of the fire listening to favourite CDs planning the days ahead, we congratulated ourselves on the hard work.

With the realisation that Rob and I had finally achieved our dream, we all raised our glasses to our little French home. "Cheers!" and "*Santé!*"

Early the next day, EDF turned on the power! What joy! There was a scrum to get into the shower first, but with plenty of hot water to go around, we were finally able to wash off the grime from the previous two days. It was sheer bliss to feel clean at last. A boiled kettle and a sink just didn't do the job!

Chapter 7
SNOW, SCENERY AND SITE SEEING

After all the hard work, showered and smelling delightful, we decided to take some time off. We deserved it. A long journey, car problems and moving in had taken their toll. Any other jobs could wait. Now it was time to explore and have some fun.

Our first outing was to buy food supplies. The village had one very small grocery store and a tiny *pâtisserie*. Both were shut. It was Monday. We decided to head to the next village further down the valley where we'd seen a sign for a supermarket. Thankfully, this was open, though it closed at 12.30 pm. It being rural France, shop opening and closing times in the villages seemed a bit hit and miss. The *pâtisserie* opened on a Sunday morning, but nothing else did. Mondays appeared to be a closing day for many and Wednesday for others. Lunchtime was sacrosanct – and still is today – with everything closing at 12.30 pm and not opening again until 3.30 pm. At least they remained open until 7.00 pm in the evening for a last minute dash if you had forgotten a vital ingredient for dinner.

It was at the supermarket where we first encountered Philippe, the butcher. It seems, from my experience of butchers, that they all tend to be 'cheeky chappies', ready to engage in banter when not too busy. Philippe was no exception. He had a tiny smattering of English that he liked to use when he had the chance and he always greeted us with a huge grin. Small in stature, with dark hair, he had one of those faces that invites humour. The light-hearted teasing went both ways, with comments flying back and forth over the counter. We always left with smiles on our faces and a bagful of delicious produce. He was very proud of his display: meat, sausages, free-range chickens and guinea fowl, *patés* and a whole host of other delights. It might have been a vegetarian's nightmare, but for carnivores like us, it was pure pleasure. He also knew his stuff and he often gave advice on which cut of meat was best for a particular dish and the quantities we needed. On the wall was a chalkboard detailing the origins of the meat he sold, all of it organic and free range. Such was his popularity, that within the year, he had moved into his own shop in our village, joined by his wife and eldest son, proudly displaying his name on the sign above the door. His youngest son was not yet old enough, but it looked like his career path was well and truly planned.

On that Monday morning, after a bit of banter with Philippe and now stocked up for most of the week, the four of us headed back to our village. It was time to explore. Along the main thoroughfare, in addition to the *patisserie* and the mini supermarket we'd spotted earlier, was a well-stocked newsagents and a *pharmacie*. Larger premises contained a DIY store we knew would become the focus of our attentions once we started any house improvements and a small carwash opposite the garage meant our muddy Rangie would soon be the beneficiary of a soapy shower and rinse. Two smallish hotels seemed to be almost deserted. It being February, we suspected anyone in need of a post-Christmas break would have escaped to enjoy relaxation and cocktails on a beach in the tropics or headed off to a popular resort in the mountains to throw themselves down the ski slopes, with plenty of après ski *vin chaude* to chase away the cold. A quiet, small village, as beautiful as it was, would probably not be on many an itinerary at this time of year and we wondered how the hotels survived. The village also appeared devoid of any type of bank, but thankfully a cashpoint filled the gap and we were somewhat comforted to know we could stock up on euros when our cash was reaching desperation point. It was good to know we had everything we needed on our doorstep, but the old town was beckoning, so we crossed the road and entered through its imposing stone gateway.

There, within the solid walls, we discovered a maze of narrow streets, often bounded on each side by tall, terraced buildings, many of them pretty homes and others abandoned and shuttered, waiting for someone to discover their potential and lovingly restore them. Dotted about were stone fountains, some set against the ancient walls and others perfectly located in the centre of one of the tiny squares. The water running from them was ice cold and, we imagined, pure enough to drink from on a warm summer's day. With snow on the ground and freezing temperatures, we decided against sampling it on this visit.

"Bloody hell! That's cold," said Rob after plunging his hand in, then rapidly attempting to dry it on his jacket.

"Idiot," said Tez.

After Rob had thrust his hand in his pocket to try to restore the blood flow to his fingers, we continued. We had entered the town from the southern gateway, passing the old prison nestled into the thick wall. Strolling further, we discovered a wine cave, and a small restaurant, both closed. Meandering past the large open doors of the church, we took the opportunity to venture inside. Its age was beginning to show; the vaulted ceiling looked to be losing bits of its plasterwork and overall, the interior was fairly unremarkable, though there were several large paintings of religious significance that looked very old and the alter space was lovely. We placed a few euros into the collection box and wandered back outside.

Its spire was a different matter. It was beautifully decorated with coloured tiles in various shades of terracotta and brown. Yellow and green tiles had been used to create a pattern in the shape of the cross on two of its sides. This spire sat upon a solid looking stone tower. Through an open, arched window at the top, it was possible to spy the bells. We came to know them well as they chimed the hours and half hours, called people to service on Sundays, tolled happily in celebration and dolefully when sadness struck. Two large clock faces sat on opposite sides, one facing north and the other south; useful when wanting to know closing time is approaching or to change your watch to French time if you'd completely forgotten to do so.

As we continued further, we passed an unexpected second *patisserie* positioned on the corner of a small square and a narrow alley. The shop was miniscule but we could see the building also housed the bakery. The comforting aroma of freshly baked bread still lingered in the air as we wandered by. We made a promise to ourselves. Return as soon as possible to savour the taste of it, and capitalise on the prospect of revelling in the sweetness offered by the luscious looking pastries we could see on display through the shop window. With taste buds tickled and appetites whetted, we moved along. *La Poste*, the post office, was spotted tucked away in a narrow street that led into an open area containing a tiny bar/restaurant. A *Tricoleur* waving proudly from a wall-mounted flag pole indicated the building housing the *Mairie* and curiously, an ancient chapel, so small you might miss it, sat unobtrusively opposite the bar. Soaking up the atmosphere, peering into nooks and crannies trying not to get lost, we finally emerged via the northern gateway.

Before us, standing proud on a rocky outcrop was the fort we could see from our balcony. This was a formidable building and looked to be perfectly preserved. Surrounded by a thick wall, we imagined that any marauding hordes looking for a fight would have been quickly repelled. We had noticed too, a smaller fort to the south side of the town with only its walls remaining, but with a vantage point ensuring long distance views down the valley. The whole of the old town had retained its authenticity and we felt we had landed on a film set. "What was the history of this place?" I wondered. I was eager to know, but any research would have to wait until I returned home to the UK. Checking the time on the church clock, we decided to head back to the house. Our feet were beginning to feel the effects of trudging around in the snow. Warmth and a late lunch were beckoning.

The following day, we spread our wings and extended our explorations. A sign on the wall near the cashpoint pointed us in the direction of a nearby *cascade*. Donning snow boots and very warm clothing, we headed off, following the snowy track that led us alongside a river and through some woodland before entering a small gorge. The cliffs on both sides were vertical and the pathway started to climb slightly and get a little narrow. As none of us fancied a dip in the freezing waters of the river gushing by below, we were careful to step around any icy patches. Eventually, we came to a metal walkway slung across the water, its purpose to allow visitors to view the *cascade* in safety. What we saw astounded us. The waterfall was frozen solid. The spray it created clung to the cliff walls, frozen into a myriad of curious shapes. There were dozens of large icicles suspended from overhanging rocks and the waterfall itself was a blue tinted sheet of ice. It was breathtaking. We stood for some time, awestruck at the artistry of Mother Nature at her wintry best.

Once back at the car we ventured further up the valley. The road was twisty and narrow with high cliff walls on one side and the rushing river Verdon on the other. Passing through the large village where we'd become overly familiar with the bus stop, and continuing towards the head of the valley, the road started to climb more steeply, the river now well below us. It seemed that wherever we went in this valley, the views were spectacular. The sky was cloudless and a remarkable shade of azure blue, contrasting beautifully with the white snow glistening in the sunshine. The further we travelled the more majestic the snow-covered mountains became. We continued over small stone bridges built across streams that tumbled into the river below and hung on to our seats as we rounded the hairpin bends. There was just so much to take in and Rob did well to avoid the distraction. He also managed to avoid a French driver who was risking life and limb overtaking at speed.

"Nutter!" Rob ranted as the French car sped past and disappeared around the sharp bend. "Did you see that? God help anyone coming the other way, what a dickhead!"

With all other 'nutters' seemingly practising their driving skills elsewhere, Rob safely negotiated his way without further comment and deposited us safely in a parking area. This was the end of the road, in winter anyway, as the route would normally continue in tight switchback turns to the top of the

Col at a height of 2250 metres (7381 feet), before snaking its way down the other side. We promised we'd follow this in the summer to see where it led. For now, the snowploughs stopped their work just past the parking area and left nature to itself from that point.

Being several hundred feet higher up from our starting point and guessing the temperature would be cold enough to freeze the snot in your nose, we were a little reluctant to get out into the frigid air and sat peering through the windows which were rapidly steaming up.

"C'mon you wimps, let's get moving," said Rob.

Reluctantly leaving the warmth of the car, we braved the chill.

"Gawd it's cold," said Tez, stating the obvious.

Before us, in the valley below, was a typical small Alpine town. On a distant snowy slope we could see skiers negotiating their way to the bottom, tiny ants on a sea of white, with tall mountain peaks providing the backdrop. Dotted about were a mix of pretty chalets, small apartment blocks and a few hotels. This charming resort sat well within its environment but insultingly, drawing the eye, was a large concrete monstrosity situated on the edge of the *piste*. Looking sinister and threatening, it resembled the sombre and depressing buildings so favoured by Soviet Russia, often seen in old spy movies set behind the Iron Curtain. It was obviously an old hotel, now abandoned and left to rot, a real insult to the beautiful setting in which it sat. What the planners were thinking when they granted permission for the construction of this ugly edifice, I have no idea, but I am glad to report its destiny was settled when it was blown to pieces and it became a long forgotten memory. A modern apartment complex, with a cinema, now sits in its place, thoughtfully designed with common sense and forethought, complementing its stunning surroundings.

We lingered a few minutes more, soaking up the scenery and shivering.

"Who wants a hot drink?" I asked.

"Me!" they all replied.

We headed downhill into the busy village centre, now enlightened as to where all those February tourists lodged, noting shops, bars and restaurants along the way, eventually wandering into a bar that looked sufficiently cosy. The coffee was hot and delicious and provided some much-needed central heating before we headed back out into the cold to see what else we could discover.

Having spotted the *piste* from our viewpoint above the town, Rob and I were chuffed we'd discovered a decent slope on which to hone our modest ski techniques, but Tez and Jan remained convincingly unimpressed. We appreciate that skiing is not everybody's idea of fun, but for Tez, who often said he could never understand why people would contemplate strapping six-foot planks to their feet and slide down a mountain at speed, the inclination to participate wasn't just lacking, it was dead in the water. We tried to persuade him otherwise, but he was having none of it.

Rob and I both loved skiing having come to it quite late, in our mid-30s. After a weekend in Gloucester at the dry ski slope learning how to put on boots and skis, and more importantly, how to stop while hurtling uncontrollably down a slope at warp speed, we headed off to Austria for a 'learn to ski' holiday on real snow. I remember it being a week of thrills and laughter, glühwein and chocolate box scenery. Like all beginners, we had our fair share of wipeouts and periods of mind-numbing fear when faced with sliding down something no steeper than a molehill. Moving at the speed of a tortoise, we also avoided serious injury. Any minor mishaps were met with cheers or hoots of laughter from our ski group, depending on the quality of the acrobatic manoeuvre we'd accidentally performed. We will never forget one Irish chap, a real character, who fell headlong into a snowdrift. All you could hear were muffled cries for help, and all you could see were his two feet sticking out of the snow, with his skis still attached, looking like something from a *Looney Tunes* cartoon. Unceremoniously dragged out, with a faceful of snow, he remained completely unaffected while everyone around him had collapsed with laughter.

"Bejesus. Dat was a bit of a tumble," he said.

By the time our week in Austria ended, the skiing bug had latched on and we were well and truly bitten.

It was at the last minute, before starting our journey to France, when Rob and I decided to sling our ski gear into the trailer, hoping for the opportunity to use it. Our explorations that day had led us towards a huge *piste* map positioned at the foot of some covered steps. Peering closely, we were thrilled to discover that our little house was minutes away from the biggest ski area in the southern Alps. Tez remained unimpressed.

We achieved such a lot during the first few days that week. Our explorations had unearthed a treasure trove of delights. Simple pleasures that amused, delighted and stunned in turn, further convincing us we'd chosen the perfect spot to realise our French dream. We had explored the small, ancient villages along the valley, stumbling across a tiny train station, which we later learned serviced the *Train de Pigne,* the Pine Cone Train. This little train trundled along its narrow gauge railway line leaving behind the sparkling Mediterranean and Nice, wending its way through the picturesque mountain scenery, stopping at little villages along the way before arriving in Digne les Bains, the capital of Provence. We had stopped to mooch for kindling for the fire, scrambling through the trees next to a crystal clear stream and eaten in a tiny restaurant at the foot of the road within walking distance of the house, climbing back up the steep hill, bellies full to bursting with the taste of wine still on our tongues. We had experienced our first walk in snowshoes, clomping through the forest following the *ski de fond* trails (cross-country ski routes) and Rob and I had squeezed in a day's downhill skiing. We had worked hard and laughed a lot. Now it was time for the formal stuff to begin.

Chapter 8
MEETING THE NEIGHBOURS

Rob and I were feeling nervous as we waited for Michel. In fact, I was very nervous. A knock on the door announced his arrival; he was taking us to our first *copropriété* meeting.

At this point, I should explain what a *copropriété* is. Our little house was one of a group of eight, some terraced, two linked detached (like ours) and one fully detached. They were constructed over a year or so to the same floor area, though differed inside according to the owner's requests at the time. The land they sat upon, the access road and the area surrounding them belonged communally to us all. No one else could extend the road to other properties, park or make changes to it. It was accepted that the land immediately to the back, side or front of each property belonged to the owners, but legally this didn't hold true. This meant that if you wanted to make any changes to your little plot, you had to seek permission from the committee. Such changes might be the removal of a large tree or the construction of a BBQ, so we're not talking about employing the skills of civil engineers or architects here! In French law, a meeting was compulsory, called once a year by the head of the *copropriété*, minutes taken and accounts kept. Any damage or works on our common land were paid for out of the community pot. The committee, populated by all the householders, decided how much everyone would contribute each year ... a bit like paying the service charge on an apartment.

It was with some trepidation that we left Tez and Jan to their own devices and followed Michel as he guided us towards a house situated above ours on the hillside. We were feeling a little apprehensive, knowing we would be scrutinised closely. We were a new phenomenon being the only Brits to have ever bought in the commune. We also surmised we would have little chance of understanding a thing!

"Do not worry", Michel said. "Everyone is friendly. I will introduce you and then leave. My new property is not part of the *copropriété*," he explained.

As we entered, I was trying to hide behind Rob, shoving him in the back and forcing him forwards into the room first where a sea of faces stared in our direction. I don't know what I expected, but I needn't have worried as we were greeted warmly by eleven of our neighbours, most of whom were squashed around a large table which almost filled the tiny living area. Two individuals kindly offered us a seat, joining those who were standing. Finally, everyone was introduced and we did our best to remember who they all were. We failed miserably!

Albert was the head of the *copropriété* and Simone was his wife; they would both turn out to be wonderful people who took us under their wing, looked out for us and treated us as part of their extended family. We became so fond of them that we called them our French mum and dad. More of them later.

The table heaved with enough alcohol to equip a small

bar, plus an array of glasses and nibbles. The atmosphere was convivial and jolly (not sure if this was alcohol induced or not) but they were definitely a happy bunch. It all helped to calm the nerves, as did the large pastis Rob was offered and the *vin de citron* I was given by Simone, apparently made in-house by Albert himself. It was so nice that it disappeared rather quickly and a sharp-eyed Simone immediately offered me a refill, which I gratefully accepted. With the warmth of the alcohol surging through our veins, the meeting got under way and Rob and I were beginning to feel a lot more relaxed.

Albert called everyone to order and the minutes of the last meeting were quickly accepted. Then the business of the day commenced. Albert insisted we sit alongside him, wanting us to know he would look after us. Just one look at him and we knew we had found an ally. His demeanour and appearance was one of a cuddly grandad. He had such a friendly open face and smiled often. He would also chuckle to himself if he thought something was amusing. Every so often, during the course of the meeting, he would turn to Rob or myself and ask,

"You understand?" to which we mostly said "Non!"

"I try explain after," he said reassuringly in his broken English.

As the meeting continued, more drinks were offered and Simone rushed back and forth to her tiny kitchen, topping up the nibbles. It was a hubbub of rapid French. We sat there like deer caught in the headlights for most of it. Albert would give us the nod when we needed to raise our hands to vote, half the time with no clue what we were voting for. It didn't matter, we trusted him and besides, the votes always seemed to be unanimous. Finally, Albert was voted in again as *chef de copropriété* and Gilbert secured his position as president. With this the last agenda item, the time was noted and the meeting was formally adjourned.

Everyone hung around to finish drinks and chat. It seemed that no one in our *copropriété* lived permanently in the mountains, all the houses being *maisons secondaires*. I suppose it made perfect sense. Living as they all did in towns along the Côte d'Azur they had access to the Mediterranean and its beaches and within two hours would be sitting on the side of a mountain. Most claimed it was a real blessing in summer. The coast would become impossibly overcrowded and the temperatures stifling. It was their escape to somewhere tranquil; somewhere they could breathe more easily. We left the meeting that evening feeling relaxed and happy. All our fears and apprehension had disappeared and we were thrilled to have been accepted into our *copropriété* so easily. We felt blessed to have met such lovely people, especially Albert and Simone.

This delightful couple became a huge part of our lives over the years and there are so many tales to tell. Some will reveal themselves as our story progresses, but I feel they deserve a little introduction all to themselves so you can get to know them a little better.

Simone was born in the Alsace but Albert's feet were firmly planted in the south. For all their married life, they had lived in St Tropez. With two children of their own, their family was expanding rapidly as great-grandchildren were beginning to make an appearance. They loved their little French home in the mountains, staying there for much of the year, enjoying the peace and quiet they said, but were never bored as they often joined the locals for a game of Lotto in the village hall, or occasionally disappeared on coach trips *pour les âgées* as Simone liked to describe them. Albert contented himself by making his *vin de citron* or *vin d'orange* for *aperitif*, a bottle of which he always gifted to us. He explained that his St Tropez friends had gardens with several lemon and orange trees, producing an abundance of fruit, much of which was freely donated and gratefully received by him. He also bought huge batches of tomatoes in season from which he made jars of *passatta* that he stored in his *sous sol* (cellar) under the house. This was added to all sorts of dishes, a taste of summer during the snowy winter months.

As for Simone, we discovered she loved creating the most beautiful, hand-sewn patchwork, her stitches as tiny and neat as any sewing machine could manage. She never seemed to have time to produce anything the size of a quilt, but produced small pieces for display or for household use, such as cushion covers. We were thrilled when she gifted us one of her display pieces, which we still treasure today. Never one to rest on her laurels, she enrolled in a watercolour painting course and would proudly show us the results of her efforts. Her main focus though was Albert, whom she fussed over, as well as keeping her beady eye on what he was up to. Occasionally she would tell him off for some minor misdemeanour, or tease him with a well-timed comment. With a wonderful sense of mischief, she once used it to great effect when she sneaked alongside Albert while he was talking on the phone, armed with a tiny pair of scissors and proceeded to trim his nose hair. He looked resigned and she looked every inch the naughty schoolgirl. A hospital visit or attention to something at home would be the only thing to draw them back to St Tropez, which, they said, had become spoiled by *les riches*. They firmly laid the blame at the door of a certain cinema star who, after settling there, had unwittingly encouraged more of the rich and famous to follow suit. The friendly little fishing town they had known for most of their lives had disappeared.

"It is all about money, money, money," they said sadly, "It is not the same place anymore."

Albert loved to tell a story to a willing audience and we

were ALWAYS a willing audience! He would start slowly, checking we understood, but often became so enthusiastic he would speed up as the tale unfolded, forgetting we could barely understand. He would get to the end, laughing heartily as he delivered the punch line with Simone joining in. Rob and I would smile politely. We had lost the thread completely. As he liked to tell us these stories more than once, we would eventually put the pieces together and grasp most of what they had been about, finally able to laugh or express horror in all the right places. One story, involved the aforementioned actor, who employed Albert to build a swimming pool. Albert was skilled in creating beautiful mosaic patterns to line the pools he constructed and we presumed one was uniquely designed and built to her specifications. Albert explained the result was judged to be excellent.

Concerned that the sun was too hot and needing something to provide shade, an additional request was made to provide a roll-out canopy on the wall of the house, with the added function of still allowing her to tan beneath it. Following instructions closely, he managed to provide what was asked for, no doubt finding a material that let the sunlight filter through, so was rather put out when she complained that it leaked when it rained.

At this point in his story Albert would shake his head in disbelief and give a chuckle.

"Vous voulez des trous pour le soleil! Vous avez donc aussi des trous pour la pluie. C'est vrai n'est-ce pas?"

We would nod in agreement confirming when you want holes for the sun, you'll have holes for rain too! As he pursed his lips and rolled his eyes heavenwards, it was obvious he thought her a little stupid.

However, this wasn't the end of his tale of woe, as when the time arrived to settle the invoice, she smiled sweetly explaining payment surely wasn't necessary? Considering her extensive notoriety, giving him permission to use her name when seeking further contracts would obviously earn him far more money than she owed him and bring in far more business in the future.

Waving a pointed finger in our direction for emphasis, Albert would always conclude his story by victoriously stating,

"I say to her. Pah! It is my reputation that brings in the work. Your name will not pay the bills for the work I do for you!"

He got his money.

Simone always presumed we were fluent in French and would chat away while busying herself in the kitchen, or supplying us with bits and bobs to eat or drink. To make matters worse, she spoke with a heavy Provençal accent. In the early days, I remember one evening, enjoying an *apéritif* at their table, when Simone mentioned *pang*. I looked blankly at her and shook my head indicating I hadn't a clue what she was on about.

"*Pang*", she said, a little louder this time.

I was still none the wiser. She tutted, disappeared into her little kitchen and returned waving a baguette.

"Oh, *pain*! ... Bread" I said.

"Oui, *pang*!" she confirmed, thinking I'd lost the plot.

We had to get used to the Provençal accent pretty quickly if we were going to communicate, but Albert and, especially Simone, were a great source of learning and we got quite used to hearing it, but not necessarily understanding it. We often chided ourselves at our lack of being able to speak French properly, and accepted fluency was never going to happen, but we tried, as you will see in the next chapter.

Chapter 9
LEARNING TO SPEAK FRENCH

Initially, we were very shy at attempting to speak French. We'd had French lessons at school, but often this was dropped when exam subjects were selected. Brought up, as most kids were at our school, on a large council estate, we thought any realistic opportunity to use the language in its native country was about as likely as holidaying on the moon. Rob's French teacher was Miss Callaghan. She was young, wore short skirts and styled her hair in a bouffant - think candyfloss minus the garish colour and the stick – which was very fashionable at the time. The look required a lot of 'back-combing' to tease the hair into position, resembling the fur of a startled cat, then a light brush across the surface for a smooth look, and finished by loads of sticky hair spray to hold it in place. I have a memory of Miss Callaghan leaning over one young man's desk, focused on correcting his work, while he attempted to gently push his ruler through her bouffant, much to the amusement of the class who were holding their collective breath and fighting to control their sniggers. His attempt failed miserably and he was duly dealt with. Many of the lads in the class, full of raging hormones, had the hots for the youthful Miss Callaghan, but not Rob. It was his form teacher, Miss Thompson, endowed with a mane of flaming red hair and a trim figure who was the focus of his attentions. He might have performed better in his French exam if he'd shared his classmates' yearning for Miss Callahan's attentions but, alas, his lusty thoughts were elsewhere.

Over the years, prior to our many holidays, I would pore over a variety of 'Teach Yourself French' books, trying to drag up anything I had learned in school. Like most schools back then, the phrases learned were fairly useless; I cannot think of many situations that call for 'the cat is black' or 'the carpet is on the floor'. You can guess my French lessons stopped at a very elementary stage. The books helped a lot, and Rob and I managed to negotiate ourselves around France picking up more as we went along. We also encouraged our children to speak the language too, sending them to the campsite shop to ask for bread and other items or persuading them to play with the French children as well as the Brits. Although we were always learning new words or phrases, we both felt we needed professional help if we were really going to improve.

It was through formal learning at night classes, where we were plunged into a world of participles, infinitives and conjugations that we began to get more of a grip on the complexities of French grammar, most sending Rob into a tailspin. He learns in a more natural way by picking up and remembering phrases. On the other hand, I need to know the minutiae: how to construct sentences, how verbs work, which are regular and which irregular and so on. When our evening class ended due to lack of recruits, we, together with our remaining group of hardcore Francophiles, set up a conversation group. Our teacher was happy to continue working with us and we clubbed together to pay her. Admittedly, a lot of the class was about catching up on gossip and drinking wine, but Martine encouraged us to 'gossip' in French and was happy to introduce us to colloquialisms and quirky sayings, "*Il pleut comme un vache qui pis*" (It's raining like a pissing cow) is one example I remember for some inexplicable reason. For the tricky stuff, we were presented with several *aide memoires* that helped if your memory was up to it. Rob still hasn't a clue what it's all about, but manages nonetheless, whereas my attention to detail does cause problems because I tend to overthink it and the conversation runs away from me, leaving me floundering like a fish out of water. Rob in the meantime is happily keeping up, not worrying in the slightest about trying to fathom which tense is being used. I always say he gets his 'French ears' on more quickly than I do.

We picked up a lot of vocabulary when faced with certain situations. We nailed camping French early on. This was joined by *Dépannage* French after numerous breakdowns (the Rangie and others) and a couple of minor traffic accidents. *Vétérinaire* French entered the picture when we acquired our little Fox Terrier, Maxwell. Besides having to negotiate the requirements for his pet Passport, now and then we needed reassurance from the vet if Max became ill (which usually proved to be a false alarm as he was fine by the time we had driven the forty minutes to the surgery.) The knack was to plot what we wanted to say before leaving the house and then carefully search for the correct words in the dictionary. Putting them into a proper sentence was a tad more complicated. We must have sounded like idiots, but we somehow got the meaning across. It was when the reply came back at hyper-speed that things started to go downhill. We would stand wide-eyed with fixed smiles, our brains trying to fathom it out.

We quickly became experts at responding with *"Pouvez vous parler plus lentement, s'il vous plaît?"* Slow was good, and at least gave us half a chance.

Not long after we had purchased our little house, a short conversation between Rob and our French neighbour occurred. Daniel, who spoke at a rate of knots and, like Simone, had a heavy Provençal accent, spotted us in the village walking Max. He came over to say hello and started to chat. I hadn't a clue what he was saying. I just stood aside, smiling and looking vacant, but after a couple of minutes I could tell he thought Rob had lost the plot. Rob's ability to hear a word he *thought* he understood meant he would hazard a guess as to what the topic of the conversation might be and answer accordingly. Considering Daniel's reaction and quick exit, this was obviously a bad tactic. I imagine it went something like this.

Daniel: "How are you?"

Rob: "Well, thank you, and you?" (Good start)

Daniel: "I see you have your dog with you. What is its name?"

Rob: "Yes."

Daniel: "Your dog is called Yes?"

Rob: "Yes, Max."

Daniel: "Yesmax is a strange name"

Rob: "Yes, he is."

With scant French language skills, asking the wine waiter to recommend a bottle is fraught with danger and could be the cause of a large hole in your hard-earned holiday fund. We have dined in a relatively small and modest establishment where the waiter recommended a wine, obviously blathering about its virtues as he pointed to the label, kissing the ends of the fingers with a flourish and exclaiming *'C'est manifique!* We hadn't a clue what he was describing, but thankfully understood the astronomical figure he'd quoted. After picking ourselves off the floor, we smiled sweetly, asked to look at the wine menu and picked a much cheaper bottle. The waiter was not amused. Yet in a rather upmarket restaurant, with a very austere *Maître du Vin*, amazingly the wine recommended, the description of which flew completely over our heads again, was incredibly reasonable. Plucked from a list with eye-watering prices suited only to royalty or Premier League footballers, he had obviously witnessed the total shock pasted on our faces while we desperately scanned the wine menu trying to find a cheap *Vin de Maison.* The moral of this? Learn those numbers, it could save you a fortune.

Glugging large amounts of wine while attempting to participate in a French conversation requires avoidance at all costs. Fully aware of your limitations at the start of the proceedings, your language skills increase exponentially with each glass you swallow, until you finally convince yourself you're fluent and reality flies out of the window. To maximise the embarrassment, there is nothing like showing off to an audience, confident in your French-speaking abilities while actually sounding like a complete moron.

This happened to me when invited to a farm belonging to the uncle and aunt of French friends of ours who live in the Vendée. Arriving at the farm, we found the uncle on his tractor in the farmyard. We were welcomed with the usual round of kissed cheeks and handshakes before he disappeared into the barn. We knew we were in for a good time when he emerged a few minutes later with a bottle of Muscadet and several glasses. We presumed he had some stashed behind the hay bales in case he found himself overcome with thirst while milking the cows.

Following on from the farmyard wine tasting, and after assisting him in rounding up his herd of cows, ensuring they were snuggled in their stalls for the night, we retired to the farmhouse. We sat around an enormous table in the huge kitchen enjoying a meal of an indeterminate number of courses, all delicious, with ingredients sourced from the farm itself. A whole host of close and distant relatives turned up, so in total we numbered around fifteen, including our two children and the son of our friends.

The company was warm, friendly and incredibly interested in all we had to say. I don't think many of them had experienced meeting *les Anglais* before, at least not at such close quarters and their curiosity was piqued. The excellent Muscadet and the conversation kept flowing. Some questions aimed at us were quite difficult to answer considering our novice level of French.

"Why do the English have *une Reine*? After all", they said, "we got rid of our Royal family years ago."

At this point in the proceedings, I truthfully have no real recollection of how I responded. It was probably something about liking our Queen and not wishing her head removed any time soon.

The Muscadet kept on coming and our glasses regularly filled. Reminiscences and stories were shared, with everyone enjoying the conviviality. The noise and laughter increased along with the copious amounts of wine drunk and in my case, after having had more than my fair share, my alcohol-sodden brain began to convince me of my fluency in French.

"About time I joined in with the story telling," I thought.

I clearly remember launching into a rather sad tale about how, several years before, Rob had accidentally run over our cat – Robinson was the only cat we've ever really been fond of and only because he behaved more like a dog. I had the full attention of everyone, all of whom seemed to be following my sorry story with bated breath. Remember, I was rather beyond help by now, so I might have imagined this. I was determined to deliver the dreadful truth, the sad consequence of Rob's actions, in order to maximise the shock as the story ended. All eyes, although bleary, were looking at me as my tale concluded, with the punch line, dramatically delivered, that Rob had *"merde le chat!"*

Silence ensued, so silent you could have heard a mouse fart. Those present obviously needed time to digest what they had just heard. Then the laughing started, beginning with a snigger and climbing to a crescendo of roaring hysteria. It seemed to go on forever, with people wiping their eyes and slapping the table with mirth. It took a while, but eventually realisation finally dawned on me; I had stated that Rob had shit the cat! Blushing deep red with shame, my embarrassment was complete. I made it my first task, once sober, to look up the French word for murder.

On our frequent trips to France across the years, we've found ourselves cringing at the behaviour of some of our fellow countrymen who believe that all French citizens are fluent in English and if unable to understand, are obviously hard of hearing or simply stupid.

"Be a good chap and bring me a brandy would you! Madam would like a glass of your BEST white wine this time and make sure it's well chilled, the last one was bloody awful!"

Having barked this order at several decibels above normal, the waiting staff would be perplexed, other diners would be unimpressed, and so would the tourists sitting outside the café several hundred metres away, wondering what all the shouting was about. I often puzzle why it is that some people feel the need to demonstrate just how 'posh' they are by speaking louder than normal folk and in the process, treat the French like idiots.

Your average holidaymaker can be just as bad, presuming

everyone understands, speaks and writes in English. At least they tend to be more polite.

Child: "Mummy, can I have fish fingers and baked beans!"

Dad: "Can we have fish fingers and beans twice … for the kids please?"

A shrug of the shoulders and a shake of the head from the waiter will indicate he doesn't understand. Dad presumes fish fingers just aren't on the menu so perseveres.

"Harry, they don't have fish fingers, you'll have to have something else."

Harry: "But I don't WANT anything else!"

Dad, with enthusiasm: "They've got pizza Harry, you like pizza."

Harry, with a moan: "But I WANT fish fingers!"

Mum, in an exasperated voice: "Just order will you! Ellie! Come here! Leave the cat alone! Harry, will you PLEASE sit still!"

Dad, now harassed, points to pizza on the menu for the kids and having spotted *Steak Tartare*, points to it saying,

"Two please" while indicating himself and his wife.

The waiter nods his understanding.

 Mum and Dad's *Steak Tartare* is duly delivered.

"What the hell is this?" Whispered by dad as it's pushed around the plate. "I thought we'd ordered a steak in a sauce of some kind, not minced beef. My God! The meat is raw and so is the egg! Waiter! Excuse me! Can you take this back please? The chef has forgotten to cook it."

Everyone makes mistakes where food is concerned and we are certainly no different. We are not averse to trying most things on a menu and have really enjoyed frogs' legs and snails, and still do. On one occasion Rob and I ordered *Langue de Bœuf*, which we guessed correctly was tongue and were willing to give it a go. Although it was cooked and sliced, it looked exactly like a tongue, recently extracted from the cow's mouth. The top surface was still rough and the underside smooth. The one end tapered to a round and the other showed the remains of its attachments. It also had a slimy and floppy consistency.

"Sorry," I said to Rob, while eyeing a slice wobbling about on the end of my fork. "I can't eat something that has spent a considerable amount of time in another mouth before mine."

We have mistaken *gibier* (game) for *gesier* (gizzards), and confused *riz* (rice) and *ris* (sweetbreads). Worse, we were once recommended to try *andouillette*, described to us as a stuffed sausage. The Wikipedia explanation describes it thus:

"True andouillette *is rarely seen outside France and has a strong, distinctive odour related to its intestinal origins and components. ... As with all lower intestine sausages, andouillettes are to some extent an acquired taste."*

Rob's more indelicate description:

"It smells like anus, tastes like shit and it's bloody disgusting!"

I agree with him!

Wikipedia isn't joking about it being an acquired taste!

Making mistakes are all part of the process so long as you learn from them. Wherever you are going in the world, we have found it is wise to learn a few phrases in the language. If anything, it will endear you to the locals who will then endeavour to bombard you with pigeon English to help you out. We have always found the French to be open and welcoming to those who try, even when the pronunciation is thoroughly mashed or words are used in the wrong context. Something we have done often and still do. We are still learning, still making embarrassing mistakes, but thankfully, moving slowly in the right direction.

Chapter 10
THE NOTAIRE'S MEETING

It was nearly the end of the week and time for our appointment with the *Notaire*. We left Tez and Jan exploring St André while we headed across to the office. Michel and Sylvanna were already waiting. We had never met Sylvanna, but we liked her instantly. She had the dark complexion and black hair of those born around the Mediterranean and was about my age. She appeared to be permanently cheerful. She laughed loudly, was fun, and I thought she was great!

I was feeling nervous. It was an important meeting and I was unsure how we would get on trying to understand the French, especially in legalese. The butterflies had started to circle in my stomach and I anxiously looked around for the nearest loo, just in case!

The door to the office opened and the *Notaire* summoned us inside. Five chairs stood in front of his large oak desk. Michelle, there to represent the *immobilier,* was already seated and the four of us occupied the remainder. Our *Notaire* then introduced himself in perfect English, informing us that his name was Claude. My butterflies immediately settled and any thoughts about desperate dashes to the toilet faded completely.

He looked to be in his thirties with dark hair and a beaming smile. He was friendly and pretty laid back, dressed casually in jeans and a jumper; no suit and tie for this young man and so different from the stiff demeanour of solicitors in the UK. Having had to pay his fee (as the buyer does in France), we hoped he hadn't been too chilled about the legal stuff and had done his job properly. We needn't have worried.

Skilfully swapping between French and English, he started by going through the *Acte de Vente* we had completed the previous October. This took forever, as he was obliged to read aloud every word of every sentence on every page! Often he would glance our way asking us to confirm details before continuing. Once concluded, he then discussed the details of the property, surveys and our legal responsibilities.

He then turned his attention to the seller information with Michel and Sylvanna. They had provided the proof confirming how much they had spent on permanent improvements to the property during their tenure. Profit made from the sale would have this amount considered when calculating any capital gains tax due. As they had owned the property for eighteen years, they would be eligible for a further tax reduction. As I write this, the rates are sitting at 78%. If the ownership of a property is for twenty-two years or more, it rises to 100%.

Once all the paperwork had been scrutinised and the finer details approved, he called us forward to sign the documents. That was it! At last, we were finally the legal owners! As this was France, glasses were distributed and a bottle of wine opened to toast the completion of the sale.

"They wouldn't do that at home," muttered Rob. "Charge you a fortune just for breathing."

Michelle offered to organise our taking over of the

insurance policy Michel and Sylvanna had taken out on the house, instruct EDF about the electricity and deal with any other necessary documentation concerning the change in ownership. We were incredibly grateful as she saved us a lot of hard work and worry.

The whole thing had taken a couple of hours and after the hand shaking and *merci beaucoups*, Claude, who turned out to be a rugby fan, playfully had a dig about England's defeat to France in the recent Six Nations match. We told Claude we would get our revenge against *les bleus* the next time the teams met, which we did of course. Pity we didn't see him again so we could crow about it. We really liked Claude, he had been efficient and amiable. His ability to swap from French to English and back again with hardly a pause was impressive.

"Wish I could do that," said Rob.

"I wonder if he's married?" I said, giving Rob a teasing grin.

"Miles too young for you" he replied, "He might be up for an offer to take you off my hands though."

"Don't be cheeky," I countered. "You'd miss me. Who'd do the decorating and wash your underpants?"

"Hmmm, you've got a point. I suppose you'd better stick around then," he said as I chased him down the stairway, trying to get hold of him.

We raced through the doors, breathless and giggling like a pair of teenagers to find Michel and Sylvanna waiting for us outside.

"Would you like to join us for dinner? Our treat." Michel said, smiling at our antics.

"We'd love to," I said, "but you don't need to pay for us."

"It is the custom. The seller always pays."

"Custom or not, it's very kind of you. We'll look forward to it." Rob responded.

The following evening we enjoyed a wonderful meal in a hotel restaurant further up the valley. The wine flowed and so did the conversation. The language barrier didn't matter in the slightest. We managed somehow, laughed our way through the meal, and thoroughly enjoyed each other's company. Saying goodbye at the end of the night, we really hoped we would see them again soon.

Reflecting on it all as our week ended; Rob and I were gobsmacked at how uncomplicated the buying process had been. We had worried so much about not knowing the language well or not being accepted into the community we were joining, but it was totally unnecessary. We had met the friendliest, most helpful people, had explored an amazing area of France and made our little French house into a home.

The morning of departure, with the packing done, the house tidied and the water drained from the pipes, we locked the door, not really wanting to leave, sadly dragging ourselves away but happily knowing we would be back soon.

"I hope this bloody car is going to get us home," I stated.

"Of course it will," Rob reassured.

Miraculously, it did.

Chapter 11
SUMMER

Rob and I were looking forward to experiencing summer in Haute Provence. We had bored the pants off everyone we knew about our little French house and our adventures so far. When in the staffroom at college, I swear my lovely colleagues feigned work, with attention fully focused on their computer screens or buried in marking, obviously avoiding my enthusiastic need to regale them with yet another 'interesting' incident, probably for the second or third time.

"Yes, Jane. You've told us that already."

I eventually got over it and concentrated on organising our next trip down. The time simply wouldn't pass by quickly enough.

By now, our 'Rangie' was history. Throughout its stay with us, and always it seemed on our trips to France, it had managed to return home on a low-loader three times. On separate visits: it overheated badly just outside St. Maxime and continued doing so until it sputtered to a stop and needed emergency medical attention. Bits had fallen off at various points on our travels and the engine seized while we were on our way to Lake Garda from southern France. On that occasion, I vividly remember struggling to cram all our camping gear into a Citröen Berlingo which was the only vehicle the insurance company could provide.

"Sorry sir, but you must appreciate it **is** August and we've no other cars left."

Thankfully, our son Ben and his family had accompanied us on holiday that year. Their car was stuffed with their own camping gear, but by swapping things around and folding down the seats, we managed to get everything in, apart from the passengers. Our son's partner, Nikki, somehow managed to squeeze into a minute gap in the Berlingo with her face pressed against the side window. She clung on for dear life. Meanwhile, our three-year-old granddaughter spent the entire journey in the front passenger seat of her dad's car, securely strapped into her booster seat, the only human in our party small enough to fit the gap.

The Berlingo remained with us until we hit the port where the camping gear had to be unloaded. Another car would be waiting for us in Portsmouth. I so regret not having photographic evidence of our little family standing around a huge heap of luggage and camping gear, abandoned on the dockside, scratching our heads and wondering how the hell we were going to get this lot onto the ferry.

With our granddaughter out of the passenger seat of her dad's car, the plan was to attempt a miracle and force a little more into the tiny space she had left behind. We shoved, pushed and folded, staggered at the amount we'd managed to squeeze between the floor and the roof. Eventually, after closing the passenger door, Ben proceeded to negotiate the car, very carefully onto the ferry, his face just visible and his nose almost resting on the windscreen. The remainder of him was stuck firmly; buried among the camping holiday contents of four adults and one small child.

He eventually returned to the dockside having successfully extracted himself from the car with no serious injury. Resembling a rag tag group of refugees, we dragged, pushed and carried the rest of our belongings on board. The crew kindly found us somewhere secure to dump them and our exhausted little party set off to locate the bar, knowing we'd be repeating the whole process in reverse on the other side of the Channel.

Our Rangie was always the cause of much mirth amongst friends as well as several local garages. Everyone was aware of our tales of woe and the car's refusal to get back to the UK under its own steam.

"It must have been the 'Friday' afternoon car, mate!"

This was presumably referring to the tendency for Friday afternoon workers to rush things in order to escape for the weekend. Let us not forget the garage know-it-all either.

"Wouldn't have risked that model mate, should'a gone with the 3rd Generation L322 version."

This statement would be delivered after drawing breath through his teeth while slowly shaking his head.

Hindsight is a wonderful thing.

The Rangie duly arrived home after the Berlingo debacle and was totally defunct unless it could be equipped with another engine. Through an acquaintance, Rob picked up a cheap one from a college that had used it to aid the teaching of mechanical apprentices. 'Dear God!' I thought, 'here we go again.' Despite all my warranted misgivings, it worked beautifully, but I had lost confidence in the car's ability to manage another trip to France without conking out yet again. Every bounce, bump or rattle would send me into a fit of panic, so Rob finally and thankfully sold it.

We set off that summer in our new vehicle, a second-hand

BMW estate, not exactly in the first flush of youth, but with a reasonable amount of miles on the clock and a nice guarantee from the BMW dealer. It drove like a dream and delivered us to the French house without the slightest problem.

We arrived on a sunny and hot afternoon, tired after the journey, but anxious to unpack the car and relax for the evening. Opening the shutters was a joy as the sunshine streamed in through the windows and warmed the surprisingly cool air inside the house. Outside on the balcony we took in the view we loved so much. It was our first summer and everything was in full bloom. The mountainsides were a riot of lush greens in every shade and wild Alpine flowers with jewel-like colours dotted the grassy banks. The river Verdon was hidden amidst the rich foliage. We could just about hear it as the torrents of early spring melt had now settled into a less hurried flow. The temperature was beautifully balmy, but this was no time to relax, we had a car to unpack.

A rapid check around the house revealed that everything was as we left it. A few dead flies who had failed to make an escape when we had closed the house on our last visit were swept up and binned. A couple of corpses belonging to the tiny black scorpions that sometimes venture indoors, no bigger than an earwig, followed suit. One live specimen was discovered relaxing on the kitchen floor, trying to be inconspicuous by acting dead. I wasn't fooled, so it was gently swept into the dustpan and deposited outside, in a safe place near a rocky outcrop, and left to go about its business.

Rob ventured down to the *sous sol* under the house to turn on the gas and retrieve the garden furniture. Entering the *sous sol* has always been Rob's job, my friend's job, my brother-in-law's job, my son's job; in fact, anyone's job except mine. Scorpions, beetles, earwigs, whatever, I can deal with, but the *sous sol* is prime lodging for enormous spiders. Most contrive to conceal themselves in the stonework around the inside of the entrance door, ready to jump out on unsuspecting arachnophobes like me. Wanting to be useful and help with the garden furniture, I accompanied Rob, standing outside, a good distance away from the doorway, yelling,

"Can you see any spiders?"

Rob: "No, it looks ok in here. Oh, hang on, I can see quite a large leg sticking out of a gap between the stones."

Me, shuddering, "Where exactly?"

Rob, now by the doorway and peering closely to a spot not far from his face:

"Here. Look. You can just see it. I think that leg is attached to a fairly big spider. I've got a stick here, may be if I poke it gently ....."

Me, jumping several feet backwards and nearly knocking myself unconscious on one of the balcony supports:

"YUK! Don't touch it, Don't TOUCH IT! It might crawl out and come into the house and then I'd have to leave."

I could see Rob grinning; "Now that's an idea."

Me, rubbing my sore head: "Just pass out those garden chairs and quit joking, it's not funny!"

I have no idea why I am so afraid of our eight-legged friends. My life would be a great deal easier if I could avoid freezing with fear or bouncing about like Zebedee on speed every time I encounter one. On occasion, I've had to temper my panic and evict one from our UK house. If Rob is working away and one of the hairy beasts scuttles across the carpet, I have two choices; deal with it or leave home. I can't afford to leave home so my preferred course of action is to use the glass and card method of eviction, ensuring I open the front door first so I don't have to hold the thing for more time than is absolutely necessary as the spider wriggles away inside the glass, just a few millimetres from my hand. I have been known to throw the whole lot out of the door if the spider looks like making an escape attempt just as I'm lifting the card away. Even though spiders scare the hell out of me, I can't kill one. My mum used to say, *if you want to live and thrive, let a spider run alive*, at the same time gently scooping up some huge monstrosity in her hand and gently placing it outside. Handling one would probably give me a heart attack and, I'm not brave like my mum.

Sticking with this theme for a minute, we found that our French eight-legged lodgers, in contrast to their UK counterparts, don't move very quickly, are huge, and that it is difficult finding a glass big enough to scoop them up. One winter's evening we were lazing about in front of the log fire when one huge specimen appeared from nowhere, slowly meandering up the chimneybreast without a care in the world. I froze, then attracted Rob's attention with a loud intake of breath followed by a babbled,

"Oh, my God, oh, my God, oh, MY GOD!"

He put down his book and glanced across.

"Blimey," he said. "The last time I saw one that size was in a zoo."

On another occasion, one settled beside the beer Rob had poured himself and placed on a small shelf within arm's reach of the sofa where he was sitting. I swear it was big enough to lift the glass. Even Rob shuddered, but managed to do the decent thing and put it out after finding a receptacle large enough to transport it.

Several years later, while Rob was prepping lunch in the kitchen, one landed on his head. He hadn't a clue it was a spider until he put his hand up to flick it off. The relatively large spider found itself flying through air, landing on the tiled floor. Thankfully, it was not of the enormous proportions previously mentioned and, unfortunately, it succumbed to its injuries. I didn't witness this as I was outside on the balcony and I'm not sure whether I'd have died from fright, or died laughing. I strongly suspect Rob had given a good impression of a tap dancing Fred Astaire, though he denied it of course. For several days afterwards, I closely examined the kitchen ceiling just in case ....

Back in the house, the spiders now left to their own devices in the *sous sol*, it took a couple of hours to fully settle in. I'd made up our bed in the padded cell, the nickname we gave the largest bedroom, all the 'services' were switched on and working, luggage was unpacked and stowed in the wardrobe and drawers, the fridge and food cupboards were stocked and our standby garden furniture – four plastic chairs and a plastic table – were set up.

The house required work, but we knew we had time and would achieve it bit by bit over the coming months or years. For now, we settled into our plastic chairs and contented ourselves with eating the lasagne we had bought on our journey. A simple 'bung in the oven' meal as we had no energy after the journey to slave over a hot stove. As day slipped into night, the sun slowly dipping below the mountain peaks, we happily sipped our wine while watching the swallows swooping back and forth above our heads and thanked the fates for leading us to this wonderful place.

The next morning it was hard to get out of bed until we moved aside the curtains. Dreamily, I said, "I'll never tire of waking up to that view."

"Nor me," said Rob, "but we've work to do and lazing around here isn't going to get the baby washed."

It being early morning, the fort and the small bridge over the river were still nestling in the shade, but the sun's rays had already lit the mountain peaks. As the clock ticked away, the rays gradually crept along the balcony, placing it in full sun. By mid-afternoon, it would be too hot to walk on barefoot. We dragged ourselves out of bed and started the day with breakfast outside. Rob had been down to the *pâtisserie*, returning with fresh croissants; buttery, crumbly and as light as a feather. As we ate, the only sounds were the chatter of the birds and the distant noise of a tractor in the field nearby.

With time now on our side, we could begin to make an inventory of the jobs requiring attention, measure up where necessary and decide on the materials needed. The biggest job was the roof. All the houses in our *copropriété* had been topped with shingle-type tile roofs. The harsh elements - snow and freezing temperatures in winter and blazing hot sunshine in summer- had done their worst. The tiles looked worn and, worryingly, some had even begun to fall away. They were fine for now, just, but it seemed we would need to write this job into our future budget and find a local builder to carry out the work fairly urgently.

The balcony required sanding and treating and we knew we needed an awning to provide shade, as not being skilled in walking on hot coals for fun, we needed to prevent burning the soles of our feet as the summer sun delivered its ferocious heat. The padded cell certainly needed a facelift to prevent the assault on your eyeballs. As we meandered from room to room, things requiring attention began to mount up. Outside, in the area around the house, another slew of tasks revealed themselves. Our 'to do' list was getting longer by the minute.

Our village DIY store became a useful resource for buying the annoying missing screw, washer, nut or bolt that wasn't among the thousands brought from the UK. Rob would often tell me he was popping down to the DIY store.

"Why?" I'd ask.

"I need a washer for the pipe joint."

"There are loads of washers. Think you've got every size

and shape on the planet! They're in the cupboard. Why do you need to buy one?"

"We haven't got the right size."

"For heaven's sake! You said you'd got all bases covered."

"Yeah, well ... not this one," he'd say.

"Pfft!" was all I could manage.

French DIY stuff is not cheap, and paint is so expensive you wonder if it has some kind of magical properties. It hasn't and the quality is often terrible. Buying the odd little box of screws or other small necessity from the DIY store was fine, but larger quantities or bigger items were pricey, or simply not available. Often, it was easier and more economical to drive the forty-five minutes to Dignes les Bains and visit the *Centre Commercial* or simply delay the job and buy the supplies in the UK in time for our next visit. Yet more to add to the ever growing list.

Before arriving that summer, we had arranged to have a telephone installed and had bought a handset on the way down. Technology hadn't ventured far above sea level in our part of the world. Mobile phone signals were unreliable and any chance of receiving WiFi was about as unrealistic as being beamed aboard the Star Ship Enterprise.

Simone seemed to call us more often than anybody else. One morning the phone rang. Rob was otherwise engaged, so I answered.

"Jeanne?"

"Oui."

"Simone," she announced.

Not one to beat around the bush, she came straight to the point by asking in her Provençal twang if we would like to come over for an *apéritif* that evening. I answered in the affirmative and checked the time we needed to arrive. At 6.00 pm sharp we were knocking on their door. We had taken the short cut to get there by means of a very narrow and steep, ivy-covered series of steps that went between the track running alongside our house and the track above. Simone answered the door in her pinny, happy to see us, asking how we were before ushering us inside. Albert, who had been sitting at the table, stood to greet us with a beaming smile, delivering kisses on both cheeks for me and a firm handshake for Rob. A lovely smell was wafting from the small kitchen, which turned out to be some tasty cheese pastries that Simone placed on the table alongside slices of local sausage and a selection of snacks. Much to their amusement, I had taken our large English/French dictionary along with us, which I placed in the centre of the table, just in case.

We spent far longer than anticipated at Albert's and Simone's that night. We talked for hours, quizzing each other about our lives, our families and so on. They were keen to know why we had bought our little French house and why France? We were very happy to tell them. They, in turn, were a mine of useful information about the area, our commune and its residents, and promised to introduce us to Gabriel and Marsella, the elderly farmers who lived in a large house just below us and who seemed to be related to at least half the population of the valley. The dictionary was consulted every now and again to help with the odd word or phrase. The last time we'd used it related to the considerable amount of time we spent childishly looking up swear words in both languages with our French friends who live in the Vendée. Explanations were often required to make the meaning clearer which resulted in uncontrollable giggling fits. I hasten to add, this juvenile behaviour was spurred on by the quaffing of rather a lot of wine. Thankfully, the need hadn't arisen to educate Albert and Simone in the correct meaning of the F-word or a few other choice expletives, though with their sense of humour, they wouldn't have minded at all.

These lovely people had been so warm and hospitable that when the time came to leave, I couldn't help but give them both a big hug, not generally the 'done' thing in France. Coming out onto their front steps, Albert obligingly switched on the outside light to help us navigate away from the house. After all the *pastis* and *vin de citron* consumed that night, we decided it might be a good idea to avoid the steep steps, so we took the track which wended its way around the bend, down the slope and under the branches of the willow tree. Once back, in the light of our outside lamp, we looked up to see Albert and Simone still waiting to see us safely home before going back inside and shutting their door.

Chapter 12
A BIG BIRTHDAY

Our trip this summer was timely as it was one of those years when both Rob and I reached a big birthday that ends in a nought. Rob had celebrated his earlier in the year, but mine fell while we were in France. What better time to invite our first set of guests! Four of our closest friends were due. The first to arrive were Rosi and Jeff from Key West and Rob and I drove down to pick them up from Nice airport. They had moved to the States several years before, but the Atlantic Ocean proved to be no obstacle as we saw each other regularly over the years, either when they returned to the UK to visit family, or we flew to stay with them. The following morning, Chris and Ian arrived. I had known Chris since my teenage years. She was Godmother to our children, both of whom she doted on, and was as close as any sister. Over the next couple of days, Rob and I acted as tour guides as the six of us had a riotous time.

Our first visit encompassed the Grand Canyon du Verdon. We were astonished that none of our friends had ever heard of this incredible natural phenomenon. Knowing just how spectacular it was and eager to show it off to others, we set off immediately after breakfast.

The canyon was formed by the Verdon River which carved its way through the limestone rock to become the deepest canyon in western Europe. It is 1500 metres at its widest point and 700 metres at its deepest. From 1929-1975 a series of five dams were constructed along the Verdon creating a string of reservoirs. The biggest is Lac Sainte-Croix, the largest reservoir in France, into which the waters of the river gently merge after exiting the canyon. Salles sur Verdon, a village that existed on the river plain, was sacrificed to the turquoise waters and now languishes on the lake bed. A new village of the same name was erected later to replace it, happily nestled in a spot high above the shoreline.

As we made our way around the twists and turns of the canyon, our friends were awestruck at the sheer beauty of the landscape. Choosing to journey along the *Rive Droite* we stopped at the frequent viewpoints or *belvédères*, to drink in incredible views of the turquoise blue river snaking along the canyon's depths, bordered by the tall limestone cliffs, rugged and chiselled with rock formations formed over millenia. Rob and I determined it vital to take the one way *Route de Crêtes*, running clockwise for twenty-three kilometres and perched right on the edge of the north rim. Our friends needed to experience the vertiginous view down the sheer walls of the canyon, made even more nerve-racking by the antics of rock climbers edging their way towards the top or teetering right on the edge, belaying their companion on the final part of the climb.

"My legs feel like jelly just watching them," uttered Chris.

"I think they're totally bonkers!" said Rob.

We unanimously agreed.

Leaving the climbers to it, we ventured on and finally

caught glimpses of Lac Sainte-Croix through the trees. Its clear waters, sparkling in the sunshine, acted like a magnet, drawing us towards it. We headed sharply downhill, around more twisting bends and eventually found ourselves crossing the bridge spanning the river's exit into the lake. Some youngsters were risking life and limb jumping from the middle of it into the water, narrowly missing the masses of tourists venturing into the canyon, leisurely paddling kayaks and peddling pedalos. It resembled a busy M25, only a lot more chaotic. Well, it was August when the whole of Europe was on holiday. Feeling the need to cool off, but having no swim gear with us, we satisfied ourselves by locating a quieter spot further along the shore and paddled about in the shallows before heading off to Salles sur Verdon for a well-earned drink.

As the village was a modern reconstruction, it lacked much of the atmosphere of the older towns and villages in Haute Provence and there was little of interest to hold our attention, so with our thirst quenched, we headed back. This time we followed the *Rive Gauche* which wended its way through a series of narrow tunnels carved through the rock, providing more enthralling views as we exited each one, before eventually the road turned inland, leaving the canyon behind. We finally arrived at a very busy Castellane, the popular tourist town that the Verdon river flows through before entering the canyon. The place was heaving with people, mostly Dutch from what we could hear from the accents, with an occasional Brit thrown in for good measure. Luckily finding a parking space and even more luckily, finding a restaurant that had a table available, we ate our fill of pasta and other delights. After a great day touring, we made it safely back to the house for a quick nightcap before heading to bed and sleeping like the dead.

The next day was my birthday and I awoke realising I was

entering another decade. I'm not that bothered about age and always stick to the adage that 'age is just a number' but leaping from one decade into another does cause a bit of blip in my philosophy, albeit, very short-lived. Noises emanating from below indicated that the household was awake and gearing up to face the day; time for me to do the same.

The gifts my lovely friends had brought me, along with presents and cards from home, left me feeling a tad emotional. It was all so overwhelming. Outside the house, strung between two of our plastic chairs, I then discovered a large homemade banner wishing me a Happy Big Birthday!

"Thank you, thank you," I said to Rob.

"Don't thank me," he said, "I didn't do it ... honest."

None of our friends confessed either but a shout suddenly drew our attention to Albert and Simone standing on their front steps, waving and yelling *Bon Anniversaire, Jeanne!*" Finally, the guilty party had revealed themselves and I was genuinely touched by this lovely gesture, imagining these two thoughtful septuagenarians huddled over their table, creating it just for me.

Phone calls from the 'kids' completed the perfect start to the day.

It was the time of year when the twice weekly, Provençal market was in full swing. The narrow streets of the old town squeezed in an abundance of stalls with a cornucopia of pleasures. We wandered around, absorbing the sights and smells. We sampled amazing cheeses and cured sausages, tapenades made from olives or tomatoes and tiny chunks of bread that the stallholder would dip into his olive oil for us to try. A huge van was selling langoustines the size of your fist and a huge selection of fish, so fresh, it had probably been pulled from the Mediterranean only a few hours earlier. The aroma of guinea fowls, chickens and hams roasting on spits made our mouths water and we couldn't resist adding to the already laden shopping bags with some fat, juicy white peaches.

The temptations didn't stop with the food. Clothes stalls selling Indian silk items and another displaying cool linen in sunny colours drew us girls in while the boys examined the spice and herb stall, stuffed with seemingly every one known to man. Brightly painted pottery, silver jewellery, shoes, lavender oil and even mattresses, all sold to willing customers by enthusiastic stallholders. Completely shopped out, hot and thirsty, we headed to the bar and sat outside under the shade of a parasol, supping ice-cold beers. The chiming of the church clock announced it was midday, time to head back to the house and enjoy some of the fruits of our morning's labours.

Early the next morning, the time had arrived for Chris and Ian to leave. It was a short visit, but we were immensely grateful they had made the effort to be with me on my big birthday and we wished they could have stayed for longer. There were hugs, kisses and promises to get together once we had arrived back in the UK. After we had waved them off and their car disappeared from view, the four of us headed back inside to plan the rest of our day.

Since our February visit, we discovered that the road up to the Col and beyond is closed during winter each year. This happens due to the accumulation of snow and the fact that the ski area covers much of the route. I had also carried out some research over the intervening months about the town of Barcelonnette, nestling in the valley on the other side of the Col and found, surprisingly, that it had strong connections with Mexico. A huge swathe of emigration from there to Mexico occurred in the mid-1800s. By the end of the century, they were responsible for 70% of the Mexican textile trade. Many *émigrés* eventually returned home to Barcelonnette, which sits in the Ubaye valley, building large Mexican-style homes to demonstrate their wealth and success. The links are still strong, as a Mexican Festival, complete with Mariachi bands, is held in the town each August. Although we were not in time to attend the Festival, between the four of us, it was unanimous that we undertake the journey to see this unusual town for ourselves.

We set off early, beginning the steep climb upwards around a series of sharp hairpin bends. It was strange seeing everything without an enormous covering of snow, the ski lifts now standing forlorn and empty like some strange mountain bunting, the chairs swaying gently in the breeze as they hung from their cables. The slopes, now taken over by large flocks of sheep, were carefully tended by the shepherd (*berger*) and his *patous*, better known to us as Pyrenean Mountain dogs. Written warnings reminded visitors that these dogs are not the friendly, cuddly souls you would normally encounter, but well-trained dogs that will protect the sheep from whatever they believe is danger. This can include unsuspecting tourists, so it is wise to give them a wide berth unless the shepherd is within close range.

After the stomach-churning drive, we arrived safely at the top of the Col, having managed to hang onto our breakfasts. There we found ample car parking with quite a few vehicles already in place, most disgorging hikers dressed in stout boots, carrying rucksacks. Several trails, clearly signposted, headed off in various directions, snaking away into the distance. These *randonnes* were clearly graded according to difficulty; green being the easiest and black the most difficult, suited only to the most serious enthusiasts. Standing in the early morning sunshine, with a slight chill in the pure air, we admired the amazing vistas before us. Being so high up, we had breath-taking views of the surrounding mountains, some with their lower slopes heavily forested and others covered in lush green grass with rocky outcrops and areas of scree. We spent a while admiring all of this, wandering around the grassy knolls and venturing a short way along a marked trail before returning to the car and continuing our journey.

Heading down the narrow road on the other side of the Col was certainly not suited to anyone scared of heights, as in parts the sheer drops were something to behold. The road was so narrow in places that vehicles had to slow or stop completely in order to pass each other without scraping off paintwork, losing wing mirrors or plunging over the edge. We marvelled at the views but also the cyclists, participating in France's favourite sport, struggling up some ridiculously steep inclines. We wondered what the attraction was. Seeing their faces etched with pain and effort, we puzzled at what it was that drove them to get to the top of a mountain on two wheels, under their own steam, half killing themselves in the process! Kitted out in Lycra with thighs the size of tree trunks, we could not help but admire their fortitude and sheer determination as they powered towards the top.

"Give me a motorbike any day," said Rob as we passed yet another red-faced cyclist.

It took a good hour to reach Barcelonnette, but the parking was easy enough and we spent much of the morning exploring the narrow streets, popping into shops and stopping for a coffee in the Place de la Mairie. It was a popular spot surrounded on all sides by a myriad of restaurants, their tables and chairs arranged neatly under awnings, awaiting lunchtime guests. It was far too early to start thinking about lunch, so we went in search of the Musée de la Vallée. We eventually located it and, for a small entry fee, we were able to discover a little more about the Mexican links, as well viewing a selection of sculpture and artwork. We agreed it had been an interesting visit and that Barcelonnette certainly hadn't seen the last of us.

We decided to take a different route back to the house that would take us along a high mountain pass towards the Col de Cayolle. We could then continue on, entering into the Var valley, until we hit the road taking us up and over the Col de St. Michel and back into our own Verdon valley and home. The route was glorious as it ventured through the valley, climbing steadily, eventually crossing into the Mercantour National Park. We stopped frequently to stretch legs and to take photos, pausing alongside rivers and waterfalls, wallowing in the beauty of our surroundings. We eventually reached the top where, with stomachs rumbling, we pulled in at a mountain refuge that housed basic accommodation for serious hikers. With much relief on our part, it also served food and drink. Time for a late lunch.

It was here that my friend Rosi actually acquired a plate; an old, pink, willow patterned plate. Ten minutes earlier, she had been happily eating a cheese and ham baguette from it, but she suddenly realised that one of her good friends in Key West collected the exact same china. This was confirmed after turning the plate over in order to check the maker's name. Wondering if the proprietors would sell it to her, she went over to negotiate. The proprietor looked puzzled at being confronted by a determined English lady wanting to buy an old plate, but seemed completely happy to hand the item over. One less to wash up we supposed.

"How much did you have to pay for it?" Jeff asked.

"Nothing", said Rosi, "once I'd explained why I wanted it, she insisted I have it for free. Wouldn't take a cent."

We were all genuinely surprised by this act of kindness and took photos to record the moment for posterity, especially as this momentous event had happened up a mountain in the middle of nowhere.

A couple of days later, Rosi and Jeff flew back to the States. They emailed to let us know the plate had arrived safely. If ever it turns up on the American version of the Antiques Road Show, there will be a photograph attesting to the authenticity of the story, proving that its value has nothing to do with money, but more to do with the generosity of strangers.

Chapter 13
NEW ACQUAINTANCES

Driving back from a shopping trip several days later, I spotted a notice pinned to a board next to the road at the foot of our commune. It announced the time and date of a meeting with the Mayor who, we found out, visits each of the villages and communes in the valley every year to divulge what the *Mairie* has been spending the tax revenues on and why. The residents can also raise issues and ask questions.

"Shall we go?" Rob wondered.

"No" I said. "For one we won't have a clue what's being said. Two, it'll probably be boring, and three, we won't be able to contribute even if anyone did take the slightest notice of two English interlopers."

"You've got a point," agreed Rob.

I lied, we did go, but only because Albert insisted. Once again, he was taking us under his wing by calling for and escorting us the few paces down the grassy bank to the designated meeting place. It was the most unusual of venues. No sign of formality here. No hall with chairs carefully arranged facing those representing officialdom, but a tiny open area on the street below us. The only table present was the one that had been dragged from somewhere and filled with a large quantity of booze.

"Blimey," Rob whispered, "This could be a good meeting."

The population of the commune is small at best, and that is when all those with *Maison Sécondaires* are in occupancy. Most appeared to be, but apart from us, no one else had bothered to attend, leaving it up to the locals. A very small crowd of about twenty people convened, standing quietly to hear what the Mayor had to say. He commenced by looking directly at Rob and myself. Pinned under his gaze, I didn't know what I expected. May be we had committed some faux pas, though I was positive we had paid all our bills to the *trésorie* on time. I was happily surprised and somewhat relieved when he broke into a smile and welcomed us warmly into the community. All eyes were on us as we mumbled our thanks, feeling rather embarrassed as we'd never set eyes on most of the folk there.

The Mayor then gave a speech. We had no idea what he said. Neither did we have a clue what the locals were saying in response. Our ears only pricked up when Albert mentioned *Les Anglais* and everyone laughed. We don't mind being the butt of jokes, never have, but it is nice to know what the joke is. Albert explained later. We were relieved to know it hadn't been us in the firing line, but aimed at a local who was having a go about how difficult it was to get to our commune – no idea why – something about the narrow road. Albert had shot him down in flames stating, with a hint of humour, that *Les Anglais* managed to get all the way from the UK with no problem at all and suggested the gentleman might like a heliport built in the nearby field to make things easier for him.

Once the meeting concluded, everyone crowded around the table helping themselves to what was on offer. Rob and I hung back, feeling a little unsure. This didn't last long as we had glasses of wine thrust into our hands and a queue quickly formed, with us at its head. We felt like minor celebrities as the locals waited patiently to shake our hands and say hello. One chap was really keen to talk to us and hung around to gain our full attention.

"Bonjour, et bienvenue" he said smiling "My name eez Olivier Egg and I 'ave family in UK. I am Engleesh but 'ave lived 'ere for most of my life. Sorry, my Engleesh is not good now. I want to invite you to my 'ouse for *Apéro* tomorrow."

We gratefully accepted his invitation, which seemed to please him no end. We confirmed where he lived and then attempted to make our escape, politely of course. Now in full flow, he was having none of it, enthusiastically telling us all about his relatives in the UK and how he came to be living in France. He was a lovely person and incredibly enthusiastic at meeting English people, but he hardly drew breath. We finally managed to extricate ourselves by slowly edging away, muttering something about dinner being in danger of spoiling,

"Au revoir, Monsieur Egg", I said, *"A demain."*

Once we had returned to the house, I said to Rob,

"Nice guy, but boy, he could talk. It'll be interesting seeing him tomorrow though. Great name ... sounds like something from a fairy story."

"Eh? Whadya mean?"

"Olivier Egg!"

"It's not Egg Jane, its Hague."

"Oh ... right. Well it sounded like Egg .... Oh God! I called him that when he left!"

"Well, I suppose God is an improvement over Egg," said Rob.

We were so glad we had attended the meeting. The locals were lovely, except for one inebriated character with a red face, mottled with broken veins. He slowly wandered over. Virtually standing on my toes, almost suffocating me with the alcohol fumes emanating from a mouthful of nicotine stained teeth, he proceeded to give me the once over. His bloodshot eyes were having trouble focussing, but he managed to get his vision under control when fixing his gaze on my boobs. He offered them a muttered greeting then staggered over to his mate. A conversation between them took place, during which my chest was obviously the main topic of discussion as 'Letch' (as I nicknamed him) continued to leer. I gave him the full force of my evil stare, determining he was one member of our commune I was certainly going to avoid in future.

The following evening we visited Olivier and his family as planned. They were renting the tiniest place a short walk away in the depths of our little commune. It seemed to only have one room, with a tiny kitchen at one end, a sofa and a couple of small chairs. His wife sat on the sofa with their little son, half buried in discarded clothing. Once a bottle of wine was opened and the contents distributed into small glasses, Olivier continued to share every aspect of his life with us. It was difficult to get a word in edgeways. He also demonstrated, in detail, how he had installed their little log burner and then proudly drew attention to their coffee machine, which was a new purchase he said as he showed us how it worked. He then insisted we try a coffee. They obviously hadn't a lot of money or possessions, but Olivier was such an upbeat guy and so proud of his family, we just let him get on with it. He was also keen to work and explained that he'd be willing to carry out any jobs we may want doing on the house. We said we would consider him if the opportunity arose, but wondered if he had the necessary skills. Later, we did ask him to work out some prices for us and felt bad when we had to let him down.

This all came about because of our roof, the job becoming

more urgent when, after a particularly violent storm and torrential rain, we noticed a very small leak in our bedroom coming from the top of the chimney breast where it entered the roof cavity. On our next visit to Albert and Simone's we explained our concerns. As always, they came to the rescue by telephoning the local *'charpente'*. They explained that he was a true *'artisan,'* the best in the valley and that they had used him to replace their roof. He visited the following morning.

"Bonjour, 'ello. My name is Richard and Albert asked me to come to see your roof," he said in slightly accented, but excellent English.

We invited him in, but he indicated he needed to have a closer look at the roof first, so Rob escorted Richard on his tour around the perimeter of the house, discussing what was needed, the timescales and an approximate price. He then examined inside where we showed him where the roof appeared to have leaked. With a shrug of the shoulders, he said he was unconcerned, but told us if worried to cover the beds with polythene when we closed up the house after our holiday.

Standing in the kitchen, drinking coffee, we spent quite a while chatting to this young man, finding out that he'd lived in the village all his life, was married, with two very young children. We remarked on his excellent grasp of English considering he had never been to the UK.

"It is because of my father," he said, "he was Italian and spent a lot of the war in an English prisoner of war camp. My father said he was treated very, very good and he could go to classes for the prisoners to learn English. When the war was finished, he return home, fluent in the language and he was very thankful. He love the English people, they are kind he said. He spoke often English to me and he, how you say, encourage me to learn it, but I am not fluent. I have to stop, to think of a word. Often, I make mistake."

"You sound pretty good to us. You should hear our French," I said.

"What did your Dad do for work?" asked Rob.

Richard headed for our balcony. "Come," he beckoned.

Puzzled, we followed behind.

"You see there," he said pointing to the house below on the left, "my father, he built the roof on that house, perhaps fifty years since."

He then pointed to the house directly beneath us. "That one too. It was his skill and he did many of the roofs here in the valley. All have lasted for many, many years. He taught me the skill and also his love of English people."

After this encounter, Richard became a frequent visitor. One of his hobbies was wandering around the fields further up the mountain with a metal detector. He told us he had found many ancient coins that were interesting, but not worth much. One afternoon he invited us to go with him, each of us taking a turn at sweeping the detector over parts of a muddy field. Later, with heavy hearts and dreams shattered at not finding a hoard of gold coins, we eventually gave up and returned to the house where Rob proudly displayed his treasure trove; two small Franc coins from recent times, probably lost by the farmer, one rusty nail which, according to Rob, was handmade, and a metal tag similar to the ones found in a sheep's ear. Hardly the stuff of legend. I had located nothing.

Richard also took us to places fairly near to our house where he often played as a child. Secret places that only locals knew. At one spot, about a forty-minute walk deep into our mountainous surroundings, was a rickety rope bridge suspended over a small river that flowed over huge boulders and tumbled downwards to meet the waters of the river Verdon. Further upstream from this, the river had created a small pool, its flow temporarily halted, making it a perfect spot for small children to play or for adults to sit on a rock and dangle their feet in the cool water when the summer temperatures soar.

Over the years we have often ventured to both of these spots, sometimes accompanied by our visitors, perhaps armed with a picnic, to enjoy the peace and isolation and while away a few hours with nothing to disturb the silence except the sound of the rushing water and birdsong.

As our first summer drew to a close, we were, as always, reluctant to leave and head back to the realities of work. We'd had a wonderful holiday, shared time with the best of friends, discovered more of the area and met a whole host of new people. Richard also promised that when we returned in October, the house would have a brand new weatherproof roof. He broke his promise.

Chapter 14
SHEEP AND A DISAPPOINTMENT

As summer slipped into autumn, we steadily ticked off the items on our lengthy list of things we needed to take with us on our next visit. Time flew, probably because work commitments occupied much of it. For me the first half term at college was always the toughest and Rob had found himself with jobs scattered far and wide, necessitating time away from home. We were both weary and so looking forward to a week's escape from all the stress. Therefore, it was with some excitement that we set off on our journey, thoughts now occupied with experiencing autumn in the mountains for the second time, it being the one-year anniversary of our first visit. We were also excited at seeing the new roof.

As we often do, we stopped at Bob and Sylviane's for an overnight stay. With hugs all around, a good old catch up and a wonderful meal, we left their home the following morning feeling blessed that we had such good friends in our lives and happy to be heading once more to our favourite place on the planet!

We arrived late afternoon, tired but happy. As we drove

towards the house, with eyes keen to spy our new roof, our spirits hit the floor when we saw nothing had been done and without any evidence of it starting any time soon. Our disappointment was overwhelming and it meant, with winter approaching, our old roof would, once more, be exposed to the extremes of the weather. There was a very real risk that we would face internal damage due to leaking. If Olivier was around, perhaps he would be more reliable and complete the project. It was something we would pursue within the next couple of days. For now, we pushed our disappointment aside and concentrated on settling in.

Albert and Simone always watched out for our arrival and would emerge from their house and shout a welcome to us. That evening was no different.

"*Jeanne, Rob. Bienvenue. Avez-vous fait un bon voyage et combien de temps restez-vous?*"

We yelled back that we were fine, our journey was good, but we were a little tired. We let them know we were staying for one week this time. "*On se voit demain!*" We will see you tomorrow.

"*D'accord!*" OK, they replied.

The car was loaded to the roof. I did say the list was a long one. Taking up most of the room was a large cabinet. By folding the rear seats down, we had been able to lay it flat on its back allowing us to chuck a load of smaller bits and pieces into its interior. Then closing the doors, we could carefully place less heavy items on top. We squeezed the luggage around the sides and after stopping to buy groceries on the way down, any tiny gaps that remained were stuffed to capacity. We approached the opening of the tailgate with care, it being highly likely a considerable amount of the contents would tumble out and cause serious injury. We started unloading, ferrying belongings and food back and forth into the house. The sun soon performed its disappearing act, hiding behind the mountain top and without its warmth, the temperature dropped like a stone.

"Blimey, who opened the fridge door?" I said, shivering.

"Let's just unload the essentials," suggested Rob. "We can deal with the rest tomorrow morning. Let's get in, light a fire and chill. I don't know about you, but I'm knackered."

"I knew there was a good reason I married you," I said, gratefully.

October is a fabulous time to be in the mountains. The autumn weather can be unpredictable, but one thing you never get are those leaden skies, that solid mat of grey that lingers for days on end making everyone feel depressed as the nights draw in. Here, even the dull days are interesting. Being so high up, the clouds drift in, often enveloping us in their damp mist for a time until they continue on their journey. They wrap themselves around the mountain peaks and sneak through the trees that line the mountainsides. Occasionally, they will part to show a cheery shade of bright blue, only to close ranks again and release their contents in huge drops that soak everything in minutes. We can see the rain's progress up the valley as it throws a curtain over the fort, which temporarily disappears from view. I know then that I will have a couple of minutes to retrieve any washing left drying outside before the deluge arrives. Any wet weather is generally short-lived, lasting a couple of days at most, then the morning brings cloudless blue skies and the sun dries out any evidence of the rain within minutes; the bad weather now a distant memory. The only clue will be the Verdon river, whose depths have been added to by the runoff from the mountains, turning it into a raging torrent.

October also brings with it the *transhumance*. The time when the *bergers* bring their flocks from the high peaks to lower ground before the ravages of winter set in. We experienced our first *transhumance* when driving back to the house from a trip to a village further down the valley. We came across it just outside the village and had to stop as hundreds of sheep, filling the road as far as the eye could see, were heading right for us. The *patous* were nestled within the flock, their assistance invaluable at keeping their charges heading in the right direction with some element of control. The *bergers*, some of whom were on horseback, guided the flocks, occasionally issuing a brief instruction to their loyal dogs. For drivers, it can be a nightmare, but much depends on the direction of flow. Having the sheep come towards you is better as the sheep part and trot around the vehicle, but get behind and you may be driving at a snail's pace for some time. Oh, and whatever the direction, be prepared, the need for a car wash will reveal itself once you have reached your destination.

Tradition dictates that the *transhumance* is a good reason for a celebration or festival. Our village was a little late to the party, but a brief and noteworthy event took place. Advertised in the Tourist Information Bureau, as well as on its webpage, it was described as an event set around the return of the sheep from the high pastures stating:

'Accompanying the flock, meeting with the shepherds, demonstrations, educational activities, exhibitions, film, street performances, crafts, soup of the shepherds ... are on the program of this autumn event.'

Soup of the shepherds? We hoped the poor blokes didn't have to face ritual sacrifice so they could be fed to the locals! We decided to see for ourselves.

Enclosed within the confines of a field situated below the fort, a large flock of sheep lingered patiently, happily munching on grass or standing in small groups under the shade of the trees. Five musicians dressed in traditional clothing were entertaining the crowd. Suddenly, the sheep started to move slowly as one towards the corner of the field, the folk group picked up their drum, pipes, guitar and violin and moved to take up position in front of the *troupeau.* Behind the musicians came two donkeys led by a *berger* and behind them, two more and one of the dogs. On an invisible signal, the musicians started playing a lilting tune on the pipes and the drummer beat out the timing as the procession moved slowly forward. Hundreds of sheep followed behind with more shepherds bringing up the rear. The atmospheric music, accompanied by the clanging of the bells attached to the sheep's collars, filled the air with sound as the procession moved towards the old town, entering its narrow streets through the north entrance. Joining the crowd, we headed as quickly as possible into the old town and took up position in a small street opposite the entrance to the church. The local priest, dressed in his finery, stood ready with his aspergillum (a silver ball on a stick filled with holy water) and blessed the sheep as they passed by. We hoped that the village would continue to support this spectacle every year as we felt we were witnessing something whose roots were planted in ancient times.

We are also pleased to report that all the shepherds remained alive and well.

The morning after our arrival, we finally emptied the car of its contents and decided it was time to track down Olivier. He was, as usual, very enthusiastic about fitting a new roof for us and almost immediately set to work measuring up. Within a few days, he had roughly priced everything and said he would start the job as soon as the weather improved in early spring. I liked Olivier and he was definitely an honest man with a desire to work, but I still had doubts about whether he had sufficient skill to know what he was doing. There didn't seem to be anything in his past that indicated he had had any experience of this sort and I certainly didn't want to part with lots of money for something which would look a mess or fail to keep out the rigours of the weather. Later that week, Albert and Simone invited us for the usual *apéro* and while sitting around the table, we mentioned our worries concerning Richard. We told Albert that, having not heard a thing from Richard, we had no choice but to offer the job to Olivier.

Chapter 15
OUR SECOND YEAR

As the New Year began, the roof saga had taken another turn. Unknown to us, when we had left in October, Albert had contacted Richard within a couple of days of our departure and had been quite stern with him about his lack of communication with us. He insisted that Richard identify a time to complete the work and stick to it. Within a few days of Albert's intervention, Richard sent us an itemised quote and a definite date. Because the weather was now too inclement, no work could be completed until the spring. We knew that Richard would comply this time. Albert was well known and respected within the community and had been very firm with Richard who had built an excellent reputation for the standard of his work. Up and down the valley and beyond, examples of this was evident. His artisanship showed in the roof of the church in a nearby village, tiled with those similar to the ones used on the Chapel of *Notre Dame des Grâces* in our village. Another example was a roof bizarrely styled in the shape of the upturned hull of a boat. We had no idea why his client requested this, but Richard completed it with care and skill, ensuring it stayed in keeping with its surroundings. Aside from our house and Albert's, the remaining seven would need replacement roofs quite soon, so Richard had the prospect of more work. It was a no-brainer. Richard got the job.

It was at this point that Rob had to ring Olivier and let him know our decision. We both felt terribly guilty at letting him down and he was naturally disappointed. On the other hand, he hadn't started the project and we still had not received a proper quote from him. We needed to go with the best, and that was Richard. Thankfully, Olivier didn't hold this against us and remained as friendly and chatty as ever.

Rob and I returned in the February of our second year to enjoy a week's skiing. We were guest-free and the snow was perfect. One evening, sitting by the warmth of the fire, I said to Rob, "I think I've found another dog."

"What ... Where?" said Rob, surprised.

"I've found a KC registered breeder in Ludlow and I've had an email from her. I sent her one before we left home asking if she had a litter and if any were females. She's explained all of her current litter has been sold, except for a little male and she's asked if we want to go and see him when we get back," I replied excitedly. "Sorry, but I forgot to mention it ..."

At this point, I think I should explain. Rob and I have always been dog lovers. Both of us were brought up in homes with a dog as a family pet. In my case, our dog was a mongrel called 'Tog'. My brother named her saying it was short and to the point. She also responded to 'dog', 'bog', frog or anything else that rhymed. She was brindle in colour and obviously had whippet genetics somewhere in her 'Heinz 57' mix. She was slightly larger and not quite so skinny, but boy, she was fast! She lived until she was eighteen. I'm not sure if this was down to the boiled liver my mum used to feed her, but what I do know is the smell of it bubbling away on the cooker was disgusting and I have never eaten liver since!

Rob shared some of his upbringing with a mongrel called Yogi. Yogi was often employed as co-conspirator in a number of nefarious high jinks carried out by Rob and Tez, who had apparently trained him to follow their instructions. As with large families such as theirs, a lot of this went unnoticed. Yogi was especially skilled at 'knock and run'. A length of rope was attached to his collar with a large knot tied in its end. This would be gently fed through an unsuspecting neighbour's letterbox and the dog told to sit and wait on the doorstep. Rob and Tez would hastily leg it to hide in some distant greenery. Yogi was called, the dog would obey and the knot would fly through the letterbox, clattering as it went. The neighbour would open the door to find no one there; the only thing visible would be a dog, now well distant, haring down the road trailing a length of rope. This activity, reproduced several times, continued until fate leant a hand when the knot jammed in the letterbox. The householder grabbed the rope and Yogi obediently led him to where, found hiding in a bush, were the two sniggering boys.

The pair had also trained Yogi to fetch, not the usual balls or sticks, but their younger sibling, who seemed to be a frequent target for their practical jokes. A "Yogi, fetch" would send the dog hurtling down the street and into the midst of a gang of boys, locating his target and fixing on, dragging him back towards his brothers completely unharmed, but screaming the place down while Rob and Tez were bent double laughing.

Rob's other family dog, Cindy, a boxer, had some notoriety for chewing out the entire back of their family sofa after discovering a loose thread hanging from one of the upholstery buttons. The sofa remained sitting against a wall, damage unseen, until the insurance company came to the rescue.

When married with two children, we decided to introduce dogs into the family mix. Our first was a red setter, Rhoni, who escaped from the garden and was killed as she ran across a main road. It was heartbreaking, and we all missed her dreadfully, so before long we welcomed another red setter into our home who we named Jonti. She was with us for eight years and was skilled in letterbox knocking, using her nose. She was also skilled at opening doors and cupboards. She, too, escaped and to our huge relief, a phone call informed us she had been found safe and well. Rob was dispatched to bring her back, walking to a small block of low-rise apartments, not far from our then home. Upon arrival, the young man who had telephoned explained he'd answered a knock at the door and opening it, was surprised to see this large dog sitting patiently on his doormat, calmly gazing at him with tail wagging gently. He was even more surprised when, uninvited, she casually walked passed him, down the hall and into his living room. There, she found and consumed his Sunday lunch which he had left on the coffee table while answering the door. Upon completing her meal, she curled up comfortably in front of his electric fire to digest it. The young man's friend, who witnessed all this, was apparently beside himself:

"Funniest thing I've seen in ages, mate. Hilarious!"

Having lost our wonderful Jonti to wander over the Rainbow Bridge several years later, we decided to get another dog to fill the huge gap she had left, but perhaps a smaller breed. As a child, while watching an old black and white movie I became enchanted by a dog who, in my eyes, was the best actor on the screen. It would have been a Sunday afternoon, when the TV often broadcast old movies from the 1930s and 1940s. He turned out to be Skippy, a Wire Fox Terrier who appeared in dozens of movies during the 1930s, his best-known role being that of Asta in the 1934 detective comedy, *The Thin Man*. This was the film I had been watching on that rainy afternoon. I was fascinated by Asta's antics and for me, this was the kind of dog I would have one day. Well, that day finally arrived and Rob, our children and me shared fifteen years of our lives with a Wire-haired Fox Terrier named Roxy. She was an amazing girl, full of fun and curiosity. She often took on the position of fielder when our young son was playing cricket with his mates in the street or would, if Rob was to be found in any small space carrying out DIY, push her way in to see what was going on. When visiting friends or family, she always accompanied us. As this was before the Pet Passport Scheme, we were always sad to leave her behind as we set off on our camping adventures to France, though my mum and dad, who loved her almost as much as we did, would always come and stay, caring for her until we got back.

It was now over two years since we had lost Roxy. We'd been so busy with the French house buying process and settling in, that we'd put having another dog on the back burner for a while, but as any dog lover will tell you, you can only last so long before another has to be introduced into your life. That February, and that email, led us to acquiring a bundle of Fox Terrier joy we called Maxwell.

The Pet Passport Scheme was now up and running, but back then the old rules applied. It took just over six months to complete the process before Max was awarded his passport, into which I pasted an attractive portrait of him in his neckerchief. With our next trip to France only six weeks away and legally having to wait six months, we knew we'd have to leave our new little boy at home in the care of our son.

It was Easter and we were overjoyed to see that Richard had lived up to his promise. Our new roof looked brilliant and we were comforted by the fact that it would keep the elements at bay for many years to come. Work had begun, as promised, in early spring and completed on time.

It seems we started a rash of roof replacements, as over the next few months, all the other houses, bar one, had theirs replaced too. This was much to the delight of my three girlfriends, all married and of a certain age, who happened to be on a short break with me at the house while Richard and his mate were working on a roof nearby. They delighted in ogling these two young men, who worked shirtless. Richard was definitely showing off his lean, tanned torso knowing it was attracting a certain amount of admiration. Outrageously acting up to this attention, he always gave them a cheeky smile, a little wave and a *Bonjour Mesdames* if ever he caught sight of them, while his mate simply grinned from ear to ear.

"He's a bit of all right!" they exclaimed.

"You lot are old enough to be his mother!" I chided.

"Yeah, we know, but think of it as charity. It's called helping the aged" they joked, "He's making three old ladies very happy!"

It was their first visit, arranged during the Whitsun school holiday. We usually take an annual break together, leaving our long-suffering husbands at home to enjoy some freedom from all the nagging (I'm quoting Rob here, as you can probably guess). We had flown into Nice and hired a car. The fun began when we didn't know how to start it. As the designated driver due to my friends denying any knowledge of driving in France and rigorously wimping out of trying, it was me who faced ridicule when I failed to notice the dashboard message informing me to put my foot on the brake before turning on the ignition. I blamed the fact it was in French. After leaving the airport, I also managed to get lost! My focus was on the fact the gear stick was on the wrong side of the car, along with the steering wheel, but soon mastered changing gears with my right hand without smacking my left hand into the driver's door.

A few days later, now perfectly relaxed in this new driving position, I suggested taking a picnic up to Lac d'Allos, the highest natural glacial lake in Europe, sitting at a height of 2,230 metres (7,375 feet) and nestled in the shadow of the towering Mont Pelat, one of the highest peaks in the region at 3050 metres (just over 10,000 feet). The vote was unanimous, with Gill and Eve keen to take in the scenery and Georgia, who has an obsessive interest in geology, excited to see the glacial landscape.

Just over half way up the mountain road, having negotiated numerous steep switchback turns, a burning smell began to infiltrate the interior of the car. We decided to stop. Immediately. Slap bang in the middle of the road. On a slope. We climbed out, walked around the car, sniffing it at various points trying to identify where the burning smell was coming from. A completely useless exercise as we were totally devoid of any knowledge when it came to motor vehicle maintenance and wouldn't recognise a fault if it jumped up and bit us on the bum! The sound of another car approaching halted our investigations as Gill did a great impression of a traffic cop, surprising the two incumbents who obediently stopped and rolled down the window. They appeared rather shocked as she leaned in to explain, in English, what was happening. In the meantime, I was back behind the wheel, rolling the car backwards with Eve shouting directions and waving arms around, guiding me onto a flat piece of grass at the side of the road at the bottom of the slope, out of harm's way, allowing the bemused couple to continue on their journey.

It took all of two minutes for us to realise we had no phone signal to summon help, due to the fact we were now in the depths of the National Parc de Mercantour. We hadn't a clue what was wrong with the car either, so we took the next course of action and simply abandoned it. Nothing was going to spoil our day.

After walking up the steep road to the car park and following the twenty minute climb to the top of the ridge, the girls were awestruck as they took in the view. Lac d'Allos lay in the valley below us, sparkling in the spring sunshine, its mirrored surface reflecting the mountains surrounding it. The last remnants of winter snow hung on in shady corners, the white contrasting beautifully with the blue of the icy water.

"Wow, that's amazing," said Gill and Eve, gasping in wonder. "It's stunning."

"Look", said Georgia, pointing to a lump of rock in the middle of the lake "a roche moutonnee!"

Knowing we'd probably be in for a geology lesson, we quickly changed the subject and headed down to the lake's edge to enjoy our picnic, perched on rocks which had been warmed by the sun. Afterwards, we followed the path that meandered its way around the perimeter of the lake, carefully traversing the occasional banks of snow, temporarily disturbing the peace and quiet by launching into a rendition of Edelweiss. I blame the altitude!

Later, back at the stranded vehicle, I checked the brakes were still working by rolling forwards a few feet, with the girls listening out for any grinding sounds. There were none. The burning smell was still evident, but had faded considerably, so we risked the journey back down the mountain hoping we'd not end up cremated in a ditch.

Once back in the house, I telephoned Rob back in the UK to let him know there was something up with the hire car.

"So what do you expect me to do about it? He said in disbelief. What's up with it anyway?"

"It smelt like something was hot or burning." I said.

"What did it smell like?" He said.

"Terrible!" I said.

"Twit! He said.

The clutch was assumed to be the guilty party. It hadn't appreciated my driving as I made it work harder around those switchback turns. After resting overnight, it behaved perfectly for the remainder of our stay and the car delivered us safely back to Nice several days later, in plenty of time to catch up on some serious shoe buying before our flight back to the UK.

Back to Easter ... Rob and I realised we needed to do something about changing the décor in the padded cell and install canopies over the balcony. The padded cell was the first job to deal with, as we couldn't wait to eradicate the padding and the awful over-busy patterned fabric. Giving it some thought we decided to keep it in place knowing it would be a useful insulator and fix *lambris* - wood panelling – over the top to ensure it was in keeping with the rest of the house. For the next few days we measured, sawed, nailed and glued. After a lot of hard work, the padded cell was no longer, though the hideous pattern was still evident on the curtains and inside the small walk-in wardrobe. That summer, the curtains were finally changed, but we left the wardrobe as homage to the creator!

We needed good weather to install the canopies, and this made a timely appearance. What we also needed was an awful lot of muscle. This meant Rob was appointed head builder while I stood and watched, giving him the frequent benefit of my observations and advice.

"Err ... I don't think that's level". "Doesn't look like it's in the right place."

"Really? Oh, why don't you come up here and do it then!" Replied a very grumpy Rob, trying to maintain his balance on a ladder while attempting to bolt a six-metre long metal canopy holder to the wall.

"No need to shout ... I was only saying! You can be a real miserable sod sometimes."

It wasn't long before I was called upon to give some physical assistance and so attempted to support the opposite end of the holder level, arms stretched above my head, while at the same time wobbling dangerously on a stepladder.

I was very near to dropping it when my knight in shining armour came to the rescue. This was Daniel the farmer. He must have been passing by on the road below and had heard our verbal fisticuffs and my pathetic cries. Within seconds, he'd run up the grassy bank, climbed over the balustrade, joined me on the stepladder and taken the weight from my tired arms.

"Attention, attention," Daniel said, breathing hard after his exertions. *"Je vais aider à partir de maintenant.* (I will help you now.) *C'est un travail difficile pour une femme."*

I could have kissed him ... well may be not, he wasn't my type. It was the relief of letting go and feeling the pain in my shoulders and arms drift away, not to mention avoiding the wrath of Rob if I had dropped the thing. I was so happy Daniel was going to help until the job was finished, though telling me it was too difficult for a woman, did ruffle my feathers a bit. "Pfft. What does he know," I thought. I decided to let him get away with it, partly because I didn't stand a chance of putting forward a sarcastic comment in French and because he had been kind enough to save me from probable serious injury and divorce.

In no time, thanks to Daniel's assistance, the job was complete. We offered him a beer for his efforts, but he said he had to get on. So we thanked him profusely and told him he was *"Très très gentil."* Very kind. Following this neighbourly intervention, we bumped into Daniel often and still do. He always refers to us as his *voisins Anglais* – English neighbours - and never fails to stop and say *Bonjour* if we see him out and about in town or passing by our house, waving from the road below. To this day, conversation still proves nearly impossible as we can hardly understand a word he says.

As we often frequented the various shops in the village, we found we were gradually being recognised by some of the locals who would greet us with a friendly *Bonjour* or, in the case of Richard, a dash across the road to say hello. We were touched that he introduced us to his friends as *Mes Amis Anglais*. He would often pop in for a chat and on one visit, asked if we would like to see a project, one he had been working on for some time. He loaded us into his car and drove to a village further down the valley, coming to a stop in front of a small wooden chalet, positioned in a quiet spot on the mountainside. Entering the building, he proudly showed us around explaining he and his team had built it from scratch. He had every right to be proud. It was a lovely little place, built entirely of wood with an open plan, fully fitted interior, light and airy due to the large glass doors giving views across the valley. It had taken many months to finish he told us, but his client was paying well. Rob and I gave each other a glance; now we knew why our roof hadn't materialised when promised. I suppose we couldn't blame Richard. Well-paid jobs, such as this chalet, would be rare in such a small community. Have to grab the opportunities when they arise, we thought.

Back home. The phone rang. It was Simone,

"Jeanne?"

"Oui."

"Simone: *Voulez-vous venir pour une bonne franquette ce soir? Sept heures.*"

119

"OK Simone ... *Merci.*"

I looked at Rob, explaining we had been invited for a bonne franquette.

"What's one of those?" he enquired.

"No idea." I said.

I did some research. A bonne franquette is an old expression meaning an unfussy or simple meal. It can also be a meal when several people contribute, each taking a separate dish. Simone had apparently cooked a simple one-pot meal, a little too much for just the two of them so had offered to share it with us. There was plenty to go around, which was a good thing, as Rob and I were starving. Once we'd virtually licked the pattern from our plates, hoovered up dessert and stopped behaving like greedy pigs, we sat back contentedly supping a glass of wine while Albert and Simone began to tell us one of their amusing stories. Before they had even started, they were both chuckling away at the memory. We just hoped they would remember to slow down a bit in the telling. They didn't, but between Rob and me we managed to cobble together some of it and Albert did try to explain other bits more slowly. So, here is the story, as much of it as we understood with a bit of 'gap' filling from me, about their trip to Paris, many years ago.

While staying in Paris, along with a couple of friends, they all decided to pay the Arc de Triomphe a visit, never having been there before. Starting from the Place de Concorde, they were astonished at the large crowds along the Champs Elysées. As far as they knew, nothing of importance was scheduled, so they decided to press on. Fed up with fighting the crowds on the footpath, the boys squeezed into the road where there seemed less of a crush. Albert and his mate sauntered along at a leisurely pace, chatting away, when the queue in front of them began to slow. The boys slowed too, not minding too much, as the Arc de Triomphe was now looming large. Not much further to go, they thought.

Still chatting and taking no notice of those in front, Albert was surprisingly brought to a sudden halt, nearly passing out when he found himself standing face to face with the President of France! There was a smile and a handshake before Albert was ushered along a line of dignitaries for more of the same. His friend was receiving equal attention behind him. Simone told us she and her friend had spotted earlier what was going on up ahead and had tried to attract the boys' attention before it was too late, but they were far too engrossed in their conversation to notice the frantic waving. The girls watched helplessly as Albert and his friend received the cheery smiles and handshakes from a host of important people, though exactly for what remains a mystery. They didn't hang around to find out, as once they had recovered from the shock, all four legged it, disappearing into the crowd before the gendarmes arrested them for fraudulently joining an official parade.

Chapter 16
THE MEDIEVAL FETE

It was August and Medieval Fete time in the village. The old town was, as much as possible, transformed into a medieval delight. Banners, bright with coloured stripes, were draped down its ancient walls and straw had been placed throughout the narrow streets overnight. Roving musicians, playing lilting music, meandered within the old walls, halting in small squares to entertain the crowds. A group of jesters were delighting everyone with displays of juggling and acrobatics. The main event, the *Chevaliers* - Knights - were looking suitably regal on horseback astride their magnificent horses clothed in their rider's colours. They and their accompanying squires, the word meaning 'shield bearer' in French, were surrounded by a large crowd as the knights demonstrated, with lances poised, their skills at jousting. There was much cheering as watchers were encouraged to take sides and cheer on their favourite. Later, lances now replaced by swords, the knights entered the old town, negotiating their way carefully on horseback along the narrow alleyways, dismounting from time to time for a mock fight with an opposing knight, their entourage egging on the crowd.

Market stalls thronged the straw-strewn streets. Toys based on medieval themes were proving popular as small children played with pretend swords and shields, banged drums, tried to juggle with coloured balls, or ran about, simply enjoying the novelty of being dressed in medieval garb. Hand painted glassware, leather goods, jewellery, cheeses and a variety of foodstuffs were among a whole host of things on offer. Huge vats of chicken or duck casserole were ready to feed the crowds for lunch. Squeezed between the buildings, in streets not wide enough for the smallest of vehicles, long wooden tables were set up, leaving just enough room to accommodate the diners. Restaurants were doing a roaring trade by offering 'Medieval Menus.'

The locals, the stallholders and those working in the surrounding shops were all dressed in medieval costume. The most regal were the mayor and his wife, chatting to tourists and residents alike as they strolled around the town. There were peasants and priests, princes and princesses and best of all was a pitiful creature, dressed in rags, grimy faced and pockmarked, with dirty hair springing from an even dirtier cap. Ancient footwear, full of holes poked out from beneath a scruffy robe. Bent over and pushing a tiny pram containing a dirty looking doll, this very grubby character would surprise tourists by sidling up to them, making a comment or throwing an arm around a shoulder, causing much screaming and mirth. This star of the show, a local resident we have yet to recognise without the disguise, appears every year, fully occupied with plenty of requests for photos (a selfie nowadays) from anyone brave enough to rub shoulders with this rather unsanitary looking individual.

That night the Fort was host to a medieval banquet and tickets purchased from the Tourist Information Bureau sold out quickly. Sunday would see a repeat of the previous day's entertainment and the market would be as busy as ever. The whole event drew to a close with the most magnificent firework display. This was a joy. Wandering out onto our balcony, with the Fort's floodlights switched off and the night sky inky black with just the stars and the moon to give light, we watched in wonder as the display began. With the clearest of views, we watched as fireworks soared heavenwards; spectacular rockets that exploded in multi-coloured showers, filling the sky, silhouetting the Fort and the mountain peaks. Their crackling, fizzing and hissing voices bounced around the valley and echoed towards our vantage point. We stood grinning like small children and when the last rocket had finally fizzled out, we applauded,

"That was awesome!" I exclaimed. "I can't believe our little village has just put on one of the best firework displays I've ever seen. I'm so proud of them! What a great weekend and what a way to end it."

"Amazing" said Rob "I never expected it to be like that. I was thinking may be a couple of small rockets or the odd Roman candle. How wrong can you be?"

The Medieval Fete got me thinking. Rob always says it's dangerous when I start 'thinking', worrying I might be about to dream up a job that will involve him in hard physical work or an expense of some kind. He reacts in the same way when I tell him I have had an idea, even if it's a good one. There is no pleasing some people! I was rightly curious about why our village held a Medieval Fete. Was it truly medieval and when would that have been? I hadn't a clue. Time to find out.

Here is a potted history following some fairly easy research.

The medieval timeline is a long one running from around 500 BC to the 1500s; a time of castles and crusades with many monasteries and cathedrals built during this period. Our village, originally founded by the Romans, was situated further up the mountainside from its present location, but becoming too cramped to expand, was abandoned and finally destroyed by a chap named Raymond de Turenne. Re-established in its current position at an altitude of 1200 metres between the confluence of the Lance and Verdon rivers, it became a frontier town when the towns to the north, including Barcelonnette, were given to Savoie in 1388. At this time, François 1st built the first medieval wall around the town to protect it but the design of the modern town was secured when France was at war with Savoie in 1690. It was then that Louis XIV employed Vauban, a Marshal of France and the foremost military engineer of his age. Examples of his skill in designing fortifications can still be seen all over France today. On this occasion, it was Vauban's job to draw up the plans to strengthen those at Colmars les Alpes. The wall underwent some improvements around 1692 when the two towers were erected. Later still, the two forts were constructed, also to Vauban's plans, the smaller Fort Calvaire now known as the Fort de France to the south and Fort Saint-Martin, now the Fort de Savoie, to the north.

Nowadays, the village is recognised as a site of special natural, scientific and historical interest and is an approved Villages et Cites de Caractère.

Chapter 17
THE ELDERLY FARMERS

"I want that car!" I said to Rob as we were standing on the balcony one morning, overlooking the road below. The car was an old Citröen Mehari with a removable canvas roof and open sides. The bodywork was painted a rich cream and the wheels had turquoise blue hubcaps. It also sounded like a lawnmower.

We often spied our elderly neighbours going about their business but verbal communication between us hadn't occurred and the only acknowledgement to date was a glance up towards us on the balcony. I am not convinced they could see us and put it down to them being in their 80s and probably struggling to see further than a few feet beyond their noses. They both looked like typical farming folk. They had the weathered faces of those who have spent much of their lives outdoors and they dressed in functional working attire. The only time we saw them 'poshed up' was on a Sunday when they set off at speed in the Citröen, heading to morning service. Marsella was always the driver, expertly manoeuvring the Citröen, accompanied by the crunching of gears and the sound of the spluttering engine as she encouraged it into life. The car seemed devoid of seatbelts, though I suppose they could have been present, but Marsella and Gabriel either didn't realise they were there or did not see the point of wearing them. I suspected the latter but I was wrong on both counts. The mystery was solved one morning when we spied the car parked in town. I simply couldn't resist the urge for a close-up inspection and after wandering as unobtrusively as I could towards it, I peered in. The interior was basic to say the least with a couple of knobs on the dashboard and the gear lever on the steering wheel. The seats were old, worn and looked really uncomfortable. The floor was lacking any covering and it appeared there were no seatbelts, but none of this put me off.

"It's just so cute," I exclaimed. Rob simply rolled his eyes at me and shook his head.

Marsella was as strong as an ox. We discovered this one morning when we noticed her dragging a large sofa from her house into the road. Open mouthed, we watched as she heaved, pushed and dragged it from her doorway. We wondered what she was going to do with it and nearly fell over in shock when she produced an axe, using it to break up sections of the sofa. She then pulled these apart with her bare hands, miraculously stuffing them all into the Citröen. With the sofa arms, seat cushions and the sofa back split into two pieces, now haphazardly standing proud of the vehicle, she clambered into the car and sped away, probably to the *déchetterie* – the local tip - to dispose of it all.

"I really wouldn't want to be driving behind that," said Rob. "One false move and the whole caboodle is going to fly into the air and decapitate some poor sod."

"I doubt it," I countered. "Somehow, I don't think this is the first time Marsella has squeezed a whole load of junk into that car. She seems a wily old bird and knows exactly what she's doing. Bet she and the car get back in one piece without killing anyone.

Sure enough, Marsella arrived back safely, so did the car and we didn't hear of any catastrophic road accidents. The whole episode would not have been quite so fascinating if carried out by a pair of meaty chaps, helped by access to a pickup truck, but this was a very elderly lady and her tiny, ancient Citröen. We reckoned they just breed them a lot tougher in the mountains.

Gabriel no longer had the strength or fitness of his wife and we presumed he was a little older. He shuffled slowly along using an old ski pole for support, his substitute for a walking stick, and had that deep gruff voice of an older man. When we finally did get to speak to him, it was not just his Provençal accent that made conversation difficult; we couldn't make out anything at all.

They lived with two dogs. Leika was white, scruffy-coated and of indeterminate breed. The other was a small Alsatian cross, named Angel. Both would scamper along to say hello, with tails wagging, demanding a fuss. We were perfectly happy to let them wander into the house and offer them a treat from time to time. One morning, we spied Marsella and Gabriel outside on their veranda, bent over Leika, armed with a huge pair of scissors, cutting her coat in a very haphazard way. They certainly didn't give any consideration to the final appearance, as Leika emerged from her grooming with her coat in uneven lengths, hair sticking up in all directions, looking a bit like a worn out fluffy duster. Thankfully, she didn't seem to mind her ordeal or the end result.

It seemed they'd also acquired, temporarily at least, a pet sheep. Leaning on his trusty ski pole, Gabriel would be seen slowly walking along with his sheep beside him like a faithful dog, the bell on its collar chiming gently. It was early one afternoon when we noticed him sitting on the wall just below our house, the sheep beside him. They were both there for quite a while. Gabriel was resting his chin on his hands that were atop his 'walking stick', deep in thought. His sheep stood close to his shoulder, not moving. Occasionally, Gabriel's hand would reach out and give his woolly companion a comforting scratch behind the ear and murmur something to him, his voice gruff but gentle. Seeing this wizened old farmer, demonstrating such affection for this creature was a touching thing to witness. After a while, Gabriel struggled to his feet and shuffled on his way, the sheep loyally following as they headed around the bend in the road and out of sight.

What we loved about Marsella and Gabriel, and what we learned from our observations, was that this elderly couple really cared about their animals and we were sure they had been compassionate farmers who would have treated their livestock well.

At long last the day arrived when Albert and Simone lived up to their promise, arranging for us to formally meet our farmer neighbours for the first time. We were summoned to share an apéritif that evening at Gabriel and Marsella's home at 6.00 pm. Being a couple of wimps, we arrived a little late to ensure Albert and Simone were there before us, so we'd have some hope of understanding at least five percent of the conversation. The house we now found ourselves in was large and roomy, the décor a little tired and old fashioned, but it felt homely. Stretched across one side were large windows providing plenty of natural light to relieve the gloom created by the dark heavy furniture. They also afforded a great view of the valley.

Albert introduced us and indicated for us to sit at the large table, set with a selection of drinks and snacks. As we nibbled and drank, we sat quietly listening to our four elderly neighbours chatting away as old friends do. Once again, we struggled to comprehend and, once again, Albert would try to help, periodically asking if we had understood. Using simple French and limited English, he would try to explain, but often this proved difficult and we would stare at him blankly, then turn and give Gabriel a wide smile and a nod of the head, trying to convince him we knew what he was on about. It was a tad embarrassing. However, we did discover that Gabriel's grandfather had built the miniscule chapel in our commune back in the late 1800s. We had walked by this tiny building a few times, recognising it might be some kind of chapel. The size of an average garden shed and made in local stone, with a tiny arch where a small bell hung, gave a clue as to its purpose. It was sad to see it had fallen into disrepair. With a rusting roof and collapsing beams, even though the stonework remained sound enough, it was a sorry sight and we hoped that one day, the family might eventually restore it.

We also learned that Gabriel and Marsella had two sons: Daniel, our awning saviour, and an older brother we'd yet to meet. Both lived in the commune with their families, both farmed but also occupied their time with additional work. Daniel acted as the market inspector and our copropriété also employed him twice a year. His job in summer was to clear the tall grass and weeds that populated the steep banks, which he carried out with gusto, one year devastating some flowering bulbs I'd planted well away from his lethal strimmer, or so I thought! In wintertime, he, or rather his tractor, was needed to clear the deep snow that accumulated on the access road that led to our houses. Once again, his attention to detail was slightly amiss when we arrived to find he'd demolished part of a wall alongside the steps leading to our property. His enthusiasm for pushing the snow into enormous heaps knew no bounds. Our parking space was often the victim and on one occasion, he outdid himself by barricading our car and one belonging to our nephew between two enormous piles of the stuff, necessitating some back breaking shovelling to free them. His brother proved to be less of a liability as he was the deputy Mayor of the village, but his tenure only lasted until a new Mayor took over a year or two later. With their family surname so ubiquitous in the valley, it seemed there were relatives, both close and distant, scattered all over the place.

According to Simone, a female cousin of Gabriel or Marsella (no idea which) lived in the house next door to them. There appeared to have been a rather serious falling out as neither party spoke nor proffered acknowledgment when paths crossed. We reasoned familial genetics might not be shared at all and they simply disliked one another. She also had the misfortune to live with Letch, that leery individual I had run into at the Mayor's meeting, who may have had a hand in this not very neighbourly example of total disdain and indifference. Who knows? She had never spoken to anyone in the commune as far as we could see, except perhaps the postman and members of her own family.

Definitely cut from the same cloth as Marsella we watched in awe over a two-day period as she laid a floor in her garage, lugging heavy paving slabs around and fixing them into place. She was also a dab hand at cutting, splitting and stacking the truckload of tree trunks she received each summer to last her through the wintertime, something she continues to do to this present day! Uncommunicative she may be, but we do admire her strength and independence, even if it does give Rob ideas.

"You know we need those slabs re-laying at home ..."

"So?"

"Well, you could learn a lot from watching her. Save us a fortune in builders' fees."

"I hope you're not implying what I think you're implying?"

"Who? Me?"

As a happy postscript, she was obviously a sensible woman as it seemed she'd thrown out her lecherous husband a couple of years later.

As Gabriel chatted on, Rob and I were curious to know what life in the valley had been like under the occupying Germans in WWII, so we plucked up the courage and tried to ask the question using the best French we could muster. It was a minor miracle he understood. He nodded his head and seemed thoughtful for a minute, then this wizened old raconteur, keen to tell us, got into his stride and spoke for at least an hour. We had scarce understanding of what he was saying, fervently wishing we could. To hear about our valley at such a dreadful time in history, from someone who had lived through it, would have been fascinating.

We had recently seen the remains of bullet holes scarring the wall of a church in a village further down the valley. This wall was set to one side of a small square, bustling in summertime with restaurant tables laid out neatly under brightly coloured parasols and flower filled tubs placed around the perimeter. It must have looked very different during those dark times. We could only imagine the bleak and joyless place it would have been after learning about the executions of the two Frenchmen at the hands of the Germans. Amidst the happy chatter of those strolling languidly by on a sunny day, those bullet holes and plaques engraved with the names of the victims may remind those who stop, as we did, to wonder at it; to briefly remind ourselves of the horrors of war, before moving on, returning to the present and more joyful things.

Finding this sad memorial piqued our interest, and it was very frustrating that our French language skills were so sadly lacking as Gabriel's monologue was a lost opportunity to find out more. For now, our questions would have to remain unanswered. However, we did glean a tiny and rather unhappy tale involving a German soldier who deserted his unit. Not wishing to be killed in battle, Gabriel stated the man was a coward. After a lengthy search the soldier was eventually found, hiding in a cave in the mountains, and was shot for desertion. At this point, Gabriel gave a deep chuckle and simply shrugged his shoulders. He certainly showed little sympathy but we supposed that being forced to live under German occupation was at best difficult and at worst, harrowing. We continued listening to the rapid conversation as it flowed between our neighbours, catching the odd word or phrase but still missing everything in between.

When Albert and Simone finally signalled it was time to leave, we breathed a sigh of relief, not because of anything our lovely neighbours had done, but because we'd hardly uttered a word throughout and remained frustrated that we'd not been able to participate. We had so many questions for Gabriel and Marsella, but it was pointless asking them as we hadn't a hope in hell of understanding their response, especially as neither considered slowing their speech down to an understandable speed. We were completely out of our depth and determined to try to get a better grip of the French language as soon as we could. At least the time wasn't totally wasted. Marsella and Gabriel now knew who we were and acknowledged us whenever we caught their eye as they passed by on the road below, or if we bumped into them in the village.

Chapter 18
MAXWELL'S FIRST HOLIDAY

With our busy summer holiday now a distant memory, we set about organising the October visit. Maxwell the dog was now thoroughly 'passported' and could finally accompany us. We invited Tez and Janice to come too, though I had to check that Janice had no objection to sharing the back seat with Max remembering that when he was a puppy, he'd managed to pee all over her lap. She didn't and said she had forgiven him for this past misdemeanour. In the end, though, we decided to let Max travel in his crate in the rear of the car, believing it safer and knowing that he actually preferred it.

The paraphernalia a dog requires for a holiday is similar to that needed by a small child. We threw in not only the crate and cushion, but also his dog bed, bowls, leads and harness, food, treats, a towel, water for the journey, dog toys and the poo bags! The rest stops become more frequent to allow for toileting, watering and leg stretching, and not just for the dog.

Deciding to divert from our normal route through France to the house, we stopped over in Annecy. Rob and I had visited before, but it was a new experience for Tez and Jan. We wandered around the old town in the autumn sunshine, popping in and out of interesting-looking shops dotted about the narrow streets of the old town, then taking a walk alongside the sparkling Lac d'Annecy. With the trees dressed in their autumn finery, their vivid colours reflecting in the lake and with spectacular mountains as a backdrop, we marvelled at the scenery as we strolled along. Max loved it too, was impeccably behaved throughout and spoiled by everyone he met.

The French seem especially fond of Fox Terriers and sometimes they asked if we used Max for *la chasse*, the hunt. Imagining Max hunting was as far removed from reality as his ability to speak fluent French. Rabbits, foxes and even cats were treated with total disdain. The only thing he would chase was a bitch in season!

More often than not, when approached by an adult or child we would hear *"Aww, un petit Milou!"* referring to the white dog in the Tin Tin cartoons or, more seriously, *"Aww, c'est un Fox!"* Max would then bask in the adoration and allow himself to be fussed and cossetted. As the runt of the litter, Max was smaller than most male Fox Terriers and with one ear flopped over and the other standing upright, it all added to his appeal. He was a real magnet, especially for the ladies and if I left Rob standing outside a shop holding the dog on the lead, he was always surrounded with adoring females by the time I came out.

"Did you see my fan club?" He'd say, grinning.

"Dream on! Funny how they ignore you and spend the time cooing over the dog," I'd joke.

We arrived at the house the next day. Released from his crate, Max raced around as something demented, marking his territory by peeing up every upright obstacle between the car and the door to the house. He later became fascinated with a series of small drainage holes that were situated about two feet from the bottom of the enormous supporting wall that ran along the side of the track. He had once seen a gecko running into one and forever afterwards, on arrival, would jump out of the car, stand on his hind legs and stuff his nose into each drainage hole in turn. We often wondered what Max would do if a gecko actually emerged. Judging by his behaviour whenever faced with a rabbit, nothing much was our conclusion.

Our mission this October was a relatively undemanding one. We had the small job of covering up some pipework in the loo, which the boys achieved fairly quickly after buying the appropriate materials in town. Earlier, while they were happily occupied peering at interesting objects such as plasterboard in the DIY store, we girls popped in to see Philippe for a bit of banter and to buy meat supplies for the week. Philippe was his usual cheery self and we were pleased to see that his wife was no longer wearing the headscarf she'd worn the last time we had seen her. After undergoing chemotherapy for cancer and losing her hair, she chose not to wear a wig, preferring to cover her head with a gaily-coloured scarf. The scarf now consigned to the bin, she looked really well. Her hair had grown back and she was full of smiles and chat as she served us. I was enormously pleased to know that she was on the road to recovery.

Much to Philippe's delight, Rob and Tez, after their examination of boring building materials, arrived at the shop to say hello.

"Bobbeeeee!" Philippe shouted in greeting, coming around the counter to shake his hand. "Ça va?" This greeting is always the same whether Philippe is behind the counter or standing outside his shop, grabbing a couple of minutes to enjoy a cigarette. There followed one of those humorous conversations when only half of what is being said is understood by either party, but somehow the meaning is clear. Tez just stood by with a bemused look on his face, understanding nothing.

Philippe loves English beer. We discovered this when Rob took him a couple of bottles to sample one summer. It then became a bit a tradition and each time we would visit, Rob presented Philippe with a few more. We think he's become quite the connoisseur after sampling virtually every weirdly named brew Rob could find over the years. We have yet to find one he doesn't like! Trying to explain the names of some of these brews was always a bit of an ordeal. *Black Sheep* and *Spitfire* were a little less problematic than *Hob Goblin* or *Tanglefoot*, but reasoning *Bishop's Finger* as a suitable name for a beer produced a certain amount of mirth and *Sneck Lifter* proved impossible. This leaves me wondering if brewers hold meetings to come up with the most ridiculous names they can think of. I thought it would be more important to concentrate on the contents of the bottle, but not being a beer drinker, what do I know? Philippe is especially fond of one with a sensible name, produced locally to us in the UK and was quite proud when Rob told him the head of the brewing process was French.

Taking our leave, allowing Philippe and his wife to get back to their customers, we headed home for lunch in the sunshine. The boys then spent their afternoon working on the pipe-covering task while Janice and I gave them the benefit of our opinion.

The following morning, with the sun still shining, but with a definite chill in the air, we decided to drive down to Castellane and grab lunch out. Approaching Lac Castillon, we noticed that the north end of the lake was empty.

"Think someone pulled the plug out," said Tez.

It was strange and a little eerie. What had been an expanse of turquoise blue waters in the summer months was now an enormous basin of sun-baked mud. A channel running down the middle contained the river Verdon, its waters still following their original course before merging with shallow waters further along. It was somehow reassuring seeing water again as we drove over the span of the modern bridge. There, well below us, we spied the old bridge emerging into the sunlight from its watery depths, revealing ancient stones supporting a narrow road that sadly no longer led anywhere.

The lake continued to hang onto its water, deepening further as we approached the dam, but dwindling to nothing once more at the extreme southern end. It was here that we pulled into a car park and set off to explore, allowing Max a respite from the car, a good run and plenty of opportunities to cock his leg. We clambered up a small rise and noticed that part of a narrow road had been revealed on the lake bed along with another small bridge. We cautiously tested the ground and found it baked hard, the surface full of cracks created by the heat. We safely negotiated our way down and walked along this old road for a short distance, forced to stop when it reached the water level and became submerged. Halting our walk atop the small stone bridge, we sat awhile, posing for photos and gazing at the scenery around us while Max enjoyed a tentative paddle in the shallows.

It was amazing to think that in late spring and summer, this spot would be under several metres of water provided by the river Verdon and the melting snows. It would then be enjoyed by hundreds of tourists who would cool off in its crystal waters, enjoying a host of watery fun provided by the numerous pedalos and kayaks offered for hire from the beach area nearby. By the end of September, with all signs of activity packed up and gone, peace would return again. Within a short time, the process of releasing the water through the dam's turbines would begin, producing much needed electricity for homes during the coming autumn and winter and thereby reducing the water level once more.

We sauntered back to the car. The sun beat down and the autumn colours lit up the landscape. With not a soul about, we could have lingered, enjoying the tranquillity of our surroundings, but lunch beckoned, so we continued on to Castellane to enjoy a beer, a light lunch and a wander around the now deserted narrow streets. Gone were the crowds of summer with most of the shops closed and boarded up. A solitary Provençal gift shop remained open where we mooched for a while, buying small gifts for friends in the UK.

We arrived home as the sun was setting, with the temperature dropping rapidly towards freezing, but the house was warm and welcoming and with more logs on the fire, we hunkered down nursing a glass of wine each. Max curled up next to me on the sofa and there we all stayed, happily chatting about this and that, before finally heading to bed.

Chapter 19
THE VETS

During the course of the week, Rob and I realised we needed to track down a vet to administer the medication required for Max's return journey to the UK. He needed a quick health check, an application of tick solution and the prescribed tapeworm treatment, which had to include praziquantel. The vet could then complete his pet passport.

We had noticed a *Vétérinaire* sign outside a small building in the large village further down the valley and headed there to see if they could accommodate Max. Entering this tiny building, we were surprised to find it a little shabby and not very vet-like at all. The small waiting area had a stack of boxes stored along one side of the room next to the wall, with piles of discarded and dusty magazines stacked in various locations on the floor. Opposite the entrance stood a wooden reception desk that had seen better days, with the usual leaflets about animal welfare arranged haphazardly on top. Alongside these was a bell for clients to indicate they were waiting, plus one lone telephone. Behind the reception desk were a couple of shelves of randomly stored medication. A couple of nonmatching chairs were available to sit on and an animal weigh-scale completed the set up.

We could hear voices behind a closed door, but with no one official in sight and an empty waiting room, we sat down to wait, not wishing to disturb anyone by ringing the bell. We wondered if we had stumbled into a sales or storage building for veterinary practices, which would explain the absence of any animals or owners, but were soon proved wrong. A door opened and a French woman emerged with a dog that had obviously received treatment judging from the boxes of tablets the lady was carrying and the profuse thanks she was offering someone in the room. Following close behind came another women dressed in a tee shirt, jeans and trainers who wished the lady and dog an *Au revoir* as she saw her out. She then focussed her attention on us and we liked her instantly. She had such a warm smile and friendly demeanour, happily chatting away to us in rapid French, oblivious to the fact we were staring blankly or were saying *Oui* in the wrong places. This turned out to be Anita who worked as the vet's assistant, receptionist, general dogsbody and was also his wife. After showing her the pet passport and attempting to explain our needs, she nodded her understanding.

"*Bien sûr*", ok, she said. "*Un moment.*"

With that she disappeared into what we presumed to be the consultation room, spoke rapidly in French to someone we'd yet to meet, then popped her head around the door and beckoned us in.

We looked for the vet, but couldn't see one. There was a chap standing in the room who looked like a rather scruffy farmer. Over a shirt, he was wearing a very tatty jumper with a hole in the sleeve, and cargo pants. His black hair looked like it could do with a good wash and trim. Anita introduced us.

"*Monsieur le vétérinaire.*"

A little wide-eyed with surprise, we greeted him with a *Bonjour*. He nodded a greeting and gave us a small smile. He spoke little and was very serious. His consulting room clearly doubled as his office; a large desk was covered with office-type paraphernalia, plus computer. Further inside the room we spotted the consulting table where he indicated we needed to place Max. He gave the dog a quick once-over, checked eyes and ears, listened to his chest, applied the tick treatment and injected the required medication. Once done, he gave us another small smile, walked to his desk to complete the passport and finally told us how much we owed him. To say you could have knocked us down with a feather is an understatement. Rob and I tried not to indicate our shock as we handed over the cash. The whole thing has cost nine euros!

"You couldn't say 'boo' to our vet at home for that price," said Rob, later.

There was only one occasion when we needed Max treated for something other than passport requirements and that was when he had severe pain in his right ear. The poor dog would cry out if the ear was touched and we knew we needed to get him seen right away. The surgery was open. We didn't have to wait long before Anita and the vet had Max on the table. A quick examination confirmed that he was definitely suffering. What happened next was something akin to a revival of veterinary medicine from the dark ages.

Max was laid gently on his side, the bad ear uppermost. He had a cord tied around his muzzle to stop him biting and another cord was used to truss him up, with his front legs and back legs tied together to prevent him from moving. We watched on in shock as Anita held him firmly in place while the vet looked into his ear with his scope and then dug away, retrieving a small grass type seed that had been deeply imbedded. Anita spoke gently to Max throughout, stroking his fur to keep him calm and Max never uttered a sound. An injection was administered to help clear any infection and in next to no time, released from his ties, he was happily sniffing around on the floor. Once again, the fee was ridiculous and we left in disbelief, clutching the prescribed eardrops in wonder at what we had just witnessed. Max never held a grudge at his unorthodox treatment and continued to be a happy and relaxed little chap when paying a visit at passport time.

Because of our frequent visits due to the passport requirements, we grew to know Anita well. She was always happy to see us, obviously loved animals and was well travelled. She had a daughter whose university education had led to numerous work opportunities abroad. Her husband remained the shy, quiet, kind and gentle man we met on our first visit, always greeting us with a small smile, though gradually opening up a little more as time progressed. He told us he'd worked in California for a couple of years as a young vet, but admitted that nowadays, attempts to speak English were futile; he'd completely forgotten the language. He continued to wear the same jumper for years and his unkempt hairstyle never changed. Bizarrely, he never altered his method of assessing his fees, seemingly just grabbing a price out of the air. We often wondered how on earth he survived and understood why his practice lacked the usual expensive clinical surroundings and accoutrements favoured by more affluent vets.

With Max treated and passport completed, our week had reached its end and we all felt miserable at having to leave. After preparing the house for its winter shut-down, we locked up and headed for the car. After giving Max one final chance to find the gecko in the drainage pipes, we loaded him into his crate and began our long journey home.

Chapter 20
LAVENDER

Nothing symbolises Provence more than lavender; the fields clothed in vivid purple of varying shades, carefully cultivated in neat mounds and arranged in arrow-straight rows, side by side like rolls of plump carpets in a warehouse. Images adorn everything from magazine covers to tea towels. Small potpourri bags containing the fragrant dried flower heads populate every gift shop and any market worth its salt will sell lavender honey. We knew Haute Provence was famous for its lavender, but further investigation revealed there's a bit more to it. Here are a few interesting facts.

To most people, lavender is lavender, but in truth there are 47 species and most are hybrids. Haute Provence is the home of true lavender (*Lavandula Augustifolia*), growing between 500 and 1500 metres where it thrives in the less fertile soil on mountain slopes. When out on a summer walk between June and the end of August, small fragrant outcrops can be seen sprouting on sunny banks or pushing between rocks, adding a splash of colour and attracting butterflies and bees. The plant produces premium quality essential oil, with the demand leading to the region becoming one of the largest producers in the world, displaying the label PDO (the Protected Designation of Origin), guaranteeing its authenticity. The most famous area lies near the Grand Canyon du Verdon, known as the Plateau du Valensole. Here, in July and August, a sea of purple fields can be seen stretching as far as the eye can see, the air thick with heady scent. Surprisingly, this is predominantly *Lavandin*, a hybrid of true lavender and spike lavender, with its oil used in cleaning products. Small pockets of true lavender production can be seen all around the area near our little house, from a couple of small fields to postage-stamp sized plots. Here's the story of how we came across a small lavender distillery in the middle of nowhere.

It was August and Rosi and Jeff were paying their annual visit. After enjoying a lazy breakfast in the sunshine we pondered the day's activities, and settled on finding an easy 'randonée' to walk off some of the previous day's excesses. Max needed a bit of a run too. The year before, Rob and I had discovered a rough track a 20-minute drive away that twisted its way up a steep mountain slope, but we had yet to find out exactly where it led. We decided that now was the time to find out.

We set off in our new-to-us car, a lovely 4-wheel drive Discovery. (We've not had a brand new vehicle since the company car days.) Rob had been relishing the thought of taking it off-road since we drove it home from the garage a couple of years earlier, but not wanting to get the shiny paintwork muddy, I had so far managed to keep him off any roads devoid of tarmac. Today was the day I failed miserably.

Our planned walk was shelved in favour of driving up the rough track, putting our Disco through its paces. No amount of whinging from me made the slightest difference as we bounced and juddered over stones, bumped down pot holes and threw up clouds of dust as we swerved around switchback turns. Rosi was just about coping in the back, simultaneously clinging onto Max with one hand and her seat with the other, while Rob and Jeff thought the whole thing a hoot. We finally emerged onto level ground, with the track continuing to the summit where we could see a tall communications tower. For now, we stopped, parked under the shade of a mountain pine and climbed out ready to explore. Max was conducting his own explorations, sniffing about in the undergrowth and scenting tree trunks.

"See!" said Rob, looking at me with a delighted grin on his face, "Wasn't that bad was it?"

"Huh, just glad we made it here in one piece. Look at the car. It's filthy and probably scratched t'bits." I replied, somewhat grumpily.

I soon got over it as we'd arrived in a gorgeous spot with beautiful views towards the villages that nestled in the valley, which was probably the reason why some enterprising individual had created a picnic area among the trees. Wooden tables and benches had been carefully placed in the shade but the place was deserted. This didn't surprise me in the slightest considering the journey we'd just experienced to get there.

Still in need of a walk, we followed the track up to the communications tower at the summit. It was a bit of a climb and further than it looked, but we finally made it, hot and slightly out of puff, to find we had far-reaching views in the opposite direction and there, below us in the distance, we could see the tell-tale purple patches of lavender fields.

"Look!" said Rob pointing. "Can you see a track over there?"

I had a sense of what was coming next.

"Let's go see if we can find where it starts. I know you girls want to take photos of the lavender and that track looks like it's heading in the right direction."

"Oh no! Here we go again!" I thought.

After retrieving the Disco, we headed off. Rob's smile gradually faded as any chance of further macho off-roading gradually faded too; the track became a nice level surface of hard baked mud and dust. I was relaxing in blissful ignorance for at least five minutes until the track dropped away sharply onto something akin to a cliff wall. I uttered a sound similar to an owl attempting to sing opera and Rob's smile returned with a vengeance as he put the gears into hill descent saying "Now this is more like it!" Squeezed between shrubs and high banks, we made slow progress as the car would hit a deep rut and lean dangerously in one direction, then within seconds would lean the opposite way or rear up like a circus horse as the front wheels struggled over some huge boulder and slammed down the other side. With no respite, we ploughed on without a clue as to where we might end up. Injured in a ditch was my thought.

Me: "We'll never survive this. Something is bound to drop off the car and we'll be stranded in the middle of nowhere!"

Rob, with confidence: "We'll be fine, stop worrying for heaven's sake. The car is made for this. Built like a brick outhouse!"

I could cheerfully have strangled him.

Eventually the track levelled, emerging into the open as it headed towards a tiny village whose roofs we could see peeping above the brow of a hill. The boys continued to crow about how brilliant it had been; Rosi stated it wasn't that bad, but was pleased to be back on safer ground and I managed to speak in a normal voice as the tension slowly ebbed away.

After a short distance, we arrived at the lavender fields we'd spied from our lofty perch on the summit and left the car to enjoy a peaceful stroll, stopping to take photos and stooping to pick a few stems to place in the car. Clouds of butterflies in bright colours fluttered from the plants as we meandered between the rows, quickly settling again once we'd passed by. Bees flitted from plant to plant, gorging on the rich nectar, filling the air with their collective drone, the only sound to disrupt the silence, apart from the excited barks of one small dog, delighting in his freedom from the confines of the car.

It was hard to drag ourselves away, but time was getting on and we needed to find a way back. The little cluster of rooftops we'd seen belonged to the houses of a tiny settlement. Driving into a labyrinth of narrow, steep streets, we couldn't find our way out. Turning left and heading downhill, we hit a dead end, backed up and took another turn, barely able to get around the corner without demolishing the wall of a house. We continued on for a short distance, stopped and looked around; we were back where we'd started. We did this twice, taking a different route each time and still wound up in the same spot. With superb timing, a local appeared from a doorway and seemed rather bemused when we asked for directions out of there. A couple of minutes later, we escaped the maze and as we edged our way down another steep narrow road on the outskirts, we noticed a sign outside a large barn situated below us. We had stumbled across a small lavender distillery.

Checking to see if it was open, we parked next to a tractor, its trailer filled with harvested lavender plants. A young girl, who spoke reasonable English, came to greet us and said the distillery was near closing, but was willing to let us enter as a new load of lavender had just been emptied into the still. Although we were too late to watch the whole process, she was happy to explain it to us. We were very grateful and followed on behind as she led us into the interior of the barn where the aroma of lavender was so strong it made our eyes water. We were fascinated to see that this little distillery did things the traditional way as two young women were trudging around in the vat, using bare feet to break up the plants. Whether this was to make room for more plants or because it made the following process more efficient, we didn't find out but our young guide sat us on a wooden bench and proceeded to tell us what happened next. Briefly, this is what she told us.

A wooden fire is lit under a 'kettle' and the resulting steam passed through the crushed plants. The oil molecules are slowly captured in the steam as it continues to break down the plants. The steam is then passed to a condenser, where it is cooled and returned to liquid. The final process is to separate the oil from the water (the oil, being less dense, floats on top of the water), clean it and place it in jars to store for a few months.

Getting ready to leave, aware that the distillery wanted to close its doors for the day, Rosi and I were delighted when we were allowed to linger a while longer and explore the attached shop where, as well as small bottles of the pure oil, a whole host of products infused with it were displayed. With the boys looking bored stiff, Rosi and I had a happy time reading labels and choosing what to buy. We left after thanking the young woman once more and returned to the car to find Max sound asleep on the driver's seat.

Leaving the distillery parking, we turned right, as turning left would deposit us back in the labyrinth where we faced eternity going around in circles. Following the road as it snaked its way down hill, it gave us glimpses of distant mountains through the trees as we passed by dense forests populated with pine, spruce and larch on one side and near vertical rock faces on the other. The sun was behind us and the late afternoon was slowly creeping towards evening. We still had no idea where we were, but the position of the sun gave us a clue that we were heading in roughly the right direction. It wasn't long before we popped out onto the road that runs along our valley.

"Now we know where we are!" Rob and I said, simultaneously.

Forty minutes later, we were relaxing in the evening sunshine, sharing nibbles with Max and nursing G&Ts. The BBQ was lit, the salad was prepped and a bottle of local rosé wine was cooling in the fridge.

"This is just wonderful," sighed Rosi. "The perfect end to a perfect day."

Thinking back to our off-road exploits, I might have disagreed but, with hindsight, it was a bit of an adventure, just as long I didn't have to endure it again.

"Don't worry, we won't go that way again," promised Rob. He lied of course.

Chapter 21
MEETING THE BRITS

People have always been curious about our French house and its location. When we explain, most people have never heard of the village, which is completely understandable, as we had never heard of it either before buying. Others can't fathom where the Alpes de Haute Provence might be and when we tell them, we get some funny responses.

"Is it near where that bloke lives who wrote that book?" (*Well, it has got Provence in the name.*)

"Oooo, how lovely!" (*Uttered by some who pretend they know.*)

"The Alpes? That's France isn't it?" (*Obviously didn't concentrate in geography lessons at school.*)

"I wouldn't 'ave bought a house there." (*Like we care?*)

"Oh, lucky you!" (*Tinged with a mild resentment*)

"Never heard of it." (*Honesty!*)

Thankfully, most tend towards honesty and admit they have no idea. We find giving an indication of its direction and distance from Nice usually switches on the lightbulb.

It was October and Rob, on one of his forays to the DIY

store, overheard a couple in the next aisle who were obviously English. Curiosity spiked, Rob approached them and asked if they were living locally. It turned out they had bought the lovely little stone house that we could see from our balcony nestled below us in the valley. After a bit of a chat, Rob invited them for an *apéritif* that evening.

Mark and Andrea, along with their friends, Carol and Andy, who were staying the week with them, proved to be excellent company. They were over during October half–term break, partly because they were measuring up in order to make improvements to the house but also because Carol was a schoolteacher so, like me, could only escape her job during school holidays.

Brits are as rare as hen's teeth in our neck of the woods, so falling over a couple who had bought a house within screaming distance needed further investigation. We discovered their reasons were much the same as ours had been. Like us, they had visited areas nearby in the past, but it was by chance, on their last visit, that they stumbled across one of the free leaflets featuring houses for sale in the area. Scanning the listings, they spotted what looked like their dream property. A viewing was promptly organised. They had fallen for it immediately, made an offer and a few months later, the house was theirs.

Like most people meeting for the first time, everyone was on a fact-finding mission that evening, answering and asking questions about each other's lives and experiences, but as the evening progressed and the wine and beer flowed, serious conversations morphed into funny stories and there was a lot of laughter. The time flew and we suddenly realised that this *apéro* of ours was lasting much longer than anticipated. We had now been going for three and half hours. Rob and I, alerted to this by our hunger pangs and the feeling of rather a lot of alcohol sloshing around in empty stomachs, wondered how much longer we could last. We had not eaten since lunch, except for the usual nibbles we'd offered our guests. We thought we'd been sensible by preparing a meal for ourselves to enjoy after our guests had waved goodbye, but this was left abandoned on the cooker. Normally, our *apéros* went on for around two hours but that had long flown out of the window and it was gone midnight before our guests finally departed, swaying slightly as they negotiated the steps, happily stumbling their way back to their French abode in the pouring rain.

"*Au revoir* and ta-ra a bit!" a female voice shouted, shortly followed by an "Oops" and a stifled giggle. Although quite woolly-brained myself, I am sure I heard one of them singing as their voices faded into the rainy night.

After several attempts to secure the door because the lock seemed to be jumping around we suddenly remembered we were hungry and fell upon a large bag of crisps like starving lions with a downed wildebeest, devouring them in seconds.

"I'm not cooking." I said blearily, eyeing the saucepans patiently waiting on the hob.

"Nor me." said Rob. "I don't trust myself handling hot pans when I'm seeing double."

With that, we staggered upstairs to bed.

The following morning we were both slightly the worse for wear. We urgently needed rehydration. A couple of large glasses of water and a revitalising coffee gradually began to filter into our systems, the bright sunshine streaming through the kitchen window no longer burning holes in our eyeballs. My stomach however, was not a happy bunny as it began to roil and cramp; a warning sign of things to come!

"Great night," groaned Rob. "Though I think we drank enough to float the Queen Mary! Blimey, they can down it! Not sure how it got so out of hand. My tongue feels like sandpaper."

"All I know is I feel a wreck. Still, seems like everyone enjoyed themselves and we did have some great laughs." I responded, managing a small smile at the memory. "Hopefully, we'll get to meet up with them again, but let's not go overboard with the booze next time."

"What the hell is that smell?" said Rob, wrinkling his nose. "Is that you or the dog?"

"It's Max!" I responded indignantly, instantly feeling guilty as I glanced across at the sofa where our pooch was sleeping soundly, totally unaware he had just been made the prime suspect.

"Are you sure?" said Rob, eyeing me suspiciously. "You're standing a bit funny and your face looks rather pinched."

With abdominal cramps now reaching a crescendo, I turned on my heel and bolted, making it to the loo just in time.

"Fancy accusing the dog! I knew it was you!" Rob shouted after me with mock disapproval.

"Yeah? Well, *you've* never done that *have* you!" I sarcastically shouted in response.

For the remainder of the morning, the toilet became my favourite room in the house and Max received a dog treat.

As it was, we only managed to see Mark and Andrea on two other occasions simply because my college holidays didn't coincide with their visits.

Our next encounter with them was almost a year later during the summer when they invited us to an *apéritif* at their French home. It was a lovely old, detached house built in local stone with quite a large area of land at the rear. As we sat under the stars that summer night, sipping wine in a small open shelter in their garden admiring the large green space that was part of their property, their only complaint was the need to spend the first two or three days of any holiday slaving away cutting grass and removing weeds. Neither were they particularly enamoured by the fact that in autumn and winter, when the leaves had fallen from the trees surrounding their property, we could see directly into their toilet window. We thought it hysterical, but we would have needed a large telescope to get close enough to view anyone in the act of abluting!

Twelve months later, our final encounter happened when we bumped into them at the Fête of St Jean, which was held each year in the village further up the mountainside. Told about the event by Albert and Simone we decided to buy tickets and give it a go. Getting to the venue meant a trek up the steep and twisting road from the house to the very top of the commune, right on the periphery of the Mercantour Park's protected area. True, we could have driven, but that would have been lazy, especially after the huge amount of cheese, wine and bread consumed over recent days. The weather was glorious, the exercise badly needed to walk off the excess calories. Tez, Janice, their son and his girlfriend were also with us and after a certain amount of exertion negotiating the steep road, we finally arrived at the tiny village, with those less fit being out of breath, but all of us feeling the heat after the steep climb in the hot sun. We were desperate for a cold drink, but would have to exercise some patience until we discovered where to get one. The little commune consisted of no more than half a dozen houses, a small chapel and an old barn.

Presented with information about the afternoon's activities at the entrance to the Fête, we were warmly welcomed and directed into a field where large trestle tables had been organised in rows. A huge BBQ positioned alongside another series of tables, heaving with accompaniments and booze, completed the set up. It was here we encountered Mark and Andrea, along with a couple of their friends we'd not met before. Happy to see them again, we stopped for a chat before they moved away into the crowd, and with no further sightings of them, presumed they'd left after deciding an afternoon in a field with lots of French locals didn't appeal. Asking the friendly guide where we should sit, he offered us a wide smile, a sweep of his hand and the response, *"N'importe où,"*giving the six of us free range to choose for ourselves.

We settled on a vacant table nestled under the shade of the trees and marvelled at the number of people who had turned out to enjoy the feast. One of the locals was busy selling raffle tickets and the organisers were ensuring orderly queues so food would be doled out fairly. Ice cold beer and rosé wine, retrieved from large cool boxes, was being glugged with enthusiasm. At last we could quench our thirst and we each polished off an ice cold beer in seconds. It was a wonderful afternoon, sitting on long benches; cool under our leafy canopy with views towards the high mountains, surrounded by a large group of people determined to enjoy themselves to the full. Janice even won a raffle prize, a pretty, dried flower arrangement that I collected for her, she being too shy to do so.

When we said our goodbyes to Mark and Andrea that day, we didn't realise it was for the last time as we never saw them again. Whenever we made it down to our French home, they were obviously not in residence, their house being locked and shuttered. Although we thought them a lovely couple, surprisingly the locals were very disparaging in their remarks, accusing them of never trying to integrate and committing the mortal sin of using workers from the UK to help with home improvements instead of using local trades. It was a few years later when we noticed their house was for sale and it sold shortly afterwards. We have never discovered why they left.

Chapter 22
WINTERTIMES

We never missed being at the house during my February half-term. It was now our best way of getting in some skiing without the huge expense of relying on hotels and flights. Ski passes in our area were, and still are, a lot lower in price than the major resorts elsewhere in Europe, the US or Canada. We also no longer felt the need to frantically rush out to be first on the slopes and then proceed to ski ourselves to a standstill until the lifts closed. Knowing we had our house near a ski resort we also avoided the need to spend a fortune hopping on flights to Europe or across the Atlantic, where we felt obliged to ski as much as possible to justify the cost. We were also happy to welcome family and friends whenever they needed a 'snow fix'. Max the dog always came too.

Max loved the snow. We often took a day off from the slopes and took him on long walks alongside the river. He'd run around like a lunatic, burying his head in a snow bank, while sniffing out some small creature, or when trying to chase and catch snowballs. He was always a bit bewildered, wondering where this 'ball' had disappeared to as it burst into bits while trying to catch it. As he ran about, his chin, feet and leg hair became covered with frozen blobs of snow that we called *snobbles*. I have no explanation as to why they were named thus, but blame Rob who is a past master at thinking up silly names for things. Impossible to pull off his fur, we would have to put him in front of the fire for warmth where he would stand, shivering pathetically while undergoing the thawing process, eyeing us sneakily to see if we would resort to giving him a treat or wrap him in a towel. Most of the time he was pulling a fast one, his fur on the side nearest the fire would be hot, the *snobbles* now puddles on the floor, but we gave in anyway.

During our third February at the house, we had the whole family along with us and it happened that Richard popped in one late afternoon to find us all at home. We had heard on the Albert and Simone grapevine that Richard was now divorcing his wife. They had separated several months previously and she had relocated to Nice. According to the rumours, his wife had an accident prior to their split when she'd fallen out of a window while cleaning it. Simone gleefully told us her version the story. "*Non, Ce n'est pas vrai,*" she said. "It's not true. Cleaning windows? *Pah*! It is all lies! I will tell you."

Simone continued with what appeared to be some meaty gossip that had the whole village talking. You have to remember, it is a small village, so I suspect any whiff of a scandal, no matter how small, was hard come by and became a major source of entertainment. The truth appears to be that she hadn't been cleaning the window at all. She had supposedly given up smoking, but, *Quelle horreur!* appeared to be still sneakily indulging. On this occasion, she was hanging out of the window, presumably to avoid giving the game away by filling the house with cigarette smoke and was leaning so far out that she fell.

Simone thought it funny that she'd been found out, even if feeling sympathy towards her for the serious injuries she sustained, resulting in a long convalescence.

"*C'était stupide*," she stressed. "If you hang out of a window that far, you are going to fall! *Quelle folie!*"

Knowing how juicy additions can be attached to any tale through Chinese whispers, we're still not sure which bits of this are true or not!

It appeared Simone held a dislike for this lady but didn't explain why. We surmised the reason behind this when Richard introduced us to her and his lovely children when we met in the old town one morning. We were delighted to meet her, but she regarded us with a face like a bulldog swallowing a wasp, ignored us entirely and walked off. Our next meeting was also in town when she was alone. We gave her the benefit of big smiles and offered a cheery *B*onjour! She responded with a withering look and marched off without a backward glance.

"Charming, I'm sure!" I muttered as we watched her walking away.

It was sad that Richard now found himself on his own, but he saw his children often and was justifiably proud of them. Whenever we bumped into him, he remained the cheerful guy we always knew and it wasn't long before he was on the hunt for another female to share his life and his eyes temporarily focused on our daughter, Natasha.

The 'popping in' that February afternoon may not have been quite so accidental as we'd not seen him since our arrival, so the village hotline must have notified him. Richard settled himself down with a beer, stating he could only stay ten minutes or so. He got along famously with everyone, but Rob and I had to leave to attend the annual *copropriété* meeting, so left the youngsters to it. Upon our return two hours later, he was still there. Several more bottles of beer had been consumed and after a quick chat with us, he made his excuses and started to leave. We all poured outside to say our goodbyes. A farewell kiss on the cheek gifted to me, Nikki and Natasha, with handshakes for Rob and Ben. He then hovered, unwilling to get in the car just yet, finally approaching Natasha again and with a cheeky grin, demanded another couple of kisses. She politely obliged and he left smiling and waving to her from the car as he drove away. She then spent the evening subjected to unmerciful teasing about her new paramour, but she was having none of it.

"Will you lot pack it up! One, I'm not interested. Two, I wouldn't want to spend my life in a tiny village in the mountains. Three, I don't fancy him and four, more importantly, I'm completely off men and have no intention of getting involved with anyone for at least the next ten years. Been there, done that!"

She was telling the truth and stuck to her guns. She didn't settle with anyone for at least ten years, preferring to secure herself an amazing career and live life to the full. She had a cabal of great friends, backpacked around South America, had fabulous holidays and was forever out in London living the highlife. Eventually, she met and fell for a lovely Aussie guy and they are now happily settled near us in the UK and wonderfully, have presented us with two more granddaughters to spoil. Richard never forgot his encounter and made a point of asking after her whenever we bumped into him, curious to know when she would be visiting again. He was always a tad disappointed when we told him she was holidaying with friends or working hard to secure her career. After breaking the news that she had a boyfriend, the enquiries finally ceased. Mind you, I'm sure Richard wasn't entirely short of female company to keep himself occupied.

A good friend and someone we had been skiing with several times, was our guest for the week accompanied by her new husband, Trevor, who didn't ski. He seemed not to mind us disappearing for most of the day on the snow and amused himself by going for long walks with Max, meeting us in one of the cafeterias on the slopes for lunch and getting together for a drink before we all returned to the house for dinner each evening.

It was the end of the day and we had loaded our ski gear into the car and driven to a small wooden cabin at the foot of the slopes that housed a tiny restaurant and café. Elaine had gone on ahead. Pulling up outside, the door to the premises burst open and she ran out onto the steps, frantically waving and shouting to us.

"You'd better come in and deal with your dog!" she yelled, before she disappeared back inside.

"Oh God, what's he done now?" I said.

"Dunno," said Rob, "Probably disgraced himself and peed up a table leg or something. C'mon, let's go and see what all the fuss is about."

We entered the tiny eatery, where Trevor was sitting at a table. Max was, as always, thrilled to see us, jumping about on the end of his lead, tail wagging furiously as Trevor held on tightly. All seemed to be fine and we were wondering why we had been summoned so urgently. Trevor was looking a bit sheepish as Elaine was carefully negotiating her way out of the rear door to the balcony, balancing a tray of food and drink, returning several minutes later empty handed.

"Where's the food?" we asked.

"It's not for us. I've had to buy a guy a replacement meal."

"Why?"

"You'd better tell them Trevor," she said sternly.

"It weren't my fault. It were Max." said Trevor in his

Yorkshire brogue. "A bloke came in an' he were carrying his dinner an' drink on a tray. He'd also got a big dog wi' him ... he were on a lead thankfully. Max took one look an' the next thing ah knew, he'd slipped lead an' were hurtlin' towards the bloke's dog. His dog lunged at Max an' the bloke's tray went flyin'. Bugger me, there were burger an' chips all over floor, an' coffee splattered an' all. There were nowt I could do, except t'try an' grab Max, but dogs were fine by then 'cause they were 'appy hooverin' up the mess! I kept tryin' t'tell him it weren't my dog! The bloke, he were right mad. It were funny though, even boss of the place had a right old titter, an' he were the one who 'ad to clean it all up! Bloke's decided to go an' sit outside. El went an' bought 'im another dinner an' said sorry like."

Rob and I couldn't help ourselves. We didn't know whether it was the look on Trevor's face or Elaine's annoyed expression that started us off, but our suppressed giggles exploded into full-on mirth.

"It's not funny!" said Elaine, getting more annoyed by the minute, "I've had to try and calm the man down by explaining it wasn't our dog and that the owners would be here soon. It's not easy when you don't speak French! If he understood, I don't think he believed me. I tried to say sorry and in the end, I just bought him another burger. He was a miserable sod."

Elaine's annoyance just made us worse. Trevor had now joined in the hilarity. Elaine was giving us daggers, but her annoyance faded as a small smile began to tug at the corners of her mouth and before long, she was falling about like the rest of us. At Trevor's feet lay Max, drifting into a contented doze, his stomach full of burger and chips, blissfully unaware of the hullabaloo he had just caused.

Back in the car, I said to Rob, "I'd have loved to have been a fly on the wall!"

"Me too!" said Rob, laughing.

Most of our February skiing holidays were full of funny escapades resulting in fits of hysterics both on and off the slopes, but one incident was seriously worrying. The family had joined us once again and after days of enjoyment and general silliness, the laughter was suddenly silenced and panic ensued.

Ben, now a novice snowboarder, had fallen and hit his head on hard ice. He had struggled to his feet, but couldn't manage to walk steadily and eventually collapsed, but fortunately didn't lose consciousness. We received a call from Nikki, who explained what had happened, where they were located and could we get help. We hurtled down the mountain to the nearest kiosk and raised the alarm. Immediately the medics were dispatched to help. We were beside ourselves with worry, well aware of the consequences of such a fall, having heard of several deaths on the slopes over the years. We stayed in constant contact by mobile phone as the medics located Ben and transferred him to an ambulance. Nikki accompanied him, keeping us informed each step of the way. Initially he was examined by the local doctor, who, according to Ben, was rather tipsy and smelled heavily of wine, but whatever his state of inebriation the doctor thankfully decided that Ben be taken to the hospital for a head scan, just to be sure. Nikki told us that we should wait by the phone and not drive to the hospital just yet.

Back at home, the rest of us were anxiously awaiting news. A couple of hours later we received a phone call. Mercifully, the scan revealed he hadn't sustained a skull fracture or any evidence of bruising to the brain. He was fine, but shaken and needed rest. He had suffered a mild concussion, advised not to drive for a few days and to stay off the slopes. It was with huge relief that we could pick him up knowing all was well.

He emerged from the hospital wearing a huge neck brace and a prescription for medication. The pharmacy was still open, the prescription filled with enough tablets, medicines and other medical paraphernalia to keep the occupants of a small English village happy for several months. Back at the house, after enduring a fair amount of teasing on the journey back, Ben emptied the contents of his carrier bag, box by box, into a hefty pile on the table. He eventually located the box he had been searching for; the medication he was required to take immediately to help alleviate the pain. Opening the box, he struggled to take the first of two.

"These tablets are really hard to swallow," he said, holding one for us to see. "They're bloody enormous! They meant for a horse or what?"

"Oh Ben, that's priceless! They're meant for the 'other end' you nutter!" I exclaimed.

He wasn't amused, especially as the rest of us had dissolved into snort-inducing, side-splitting laughter.

All this hilarity was a joyful conclusion to a worrying day, but underlying it all was the knowledge that it could have all ended so differently. Lessons were certainly learned and since then, when on the slopes, the whole family now wears protective headgear.

Chapter 23
THE BURST PIPES SAGA

One of the perils of having a house in the mountains is the threat of burst pipes. Not being in permanent residence adds to the problem, especially over the winter when night-time temperatures can fall to an average of minus ten or below. We were warned by Gilbert that we needed to ensure the pipes were empty of water before leaving after our October stays and we were always most careful to do so, but still faced disaster when turning the water back on. The water pressure is immense, which is excellent for experiencing the sort of shower that almost pummels holes in your skin, but not so good when it's spurting several feet in the air from a pipe inside the house.

Our first burst we called the mystery leak because it took us ages to locate it. It happened upon arrival one February. Turning on the water, we waited for the rushing noise to stop as the pipes became filled to capacity, but worryingly it continued with no obvious source. After a frantic search inside and out, Rob eventually found water pouring down the wall in the *sous sol*, coming from a pipe above, situated in the shower room. I, as always, remained outside while Rob was carrying out his investigations, wondering if spiders could swim. The water was rapidly switched off and a plumber summoned.

This was plumber number one. I'm sure he hadn't anticipated just how difficult the job was going to be or how long it was going to take. He certainly earned our sympathies. By the time he left several hours later he had:

Slithered on his belly, snake like, over mud and rocks in the sous sol to access the very low space below the floor to verify the source of the leak. Returned to the shower room to remove the basin with its associated pipework, along with the base unit. Cut a hole in the inner wall enabling access to the leaking pipe. Repaired it with a hefty solder. Repaired the hole in the wall. Fixed basin, pipework and base unit back in place and cleared up the mess.

Knowing how expensive plumbers are, I was frantically checking my purse to ensure we'd enough cash to pay what was going to be a mighty sum. Rob was ready and waiting to drive to the cashpoint if my stash fell short. We were staggered when our plumber charged us less than your average call-out fee in the UK. He even refused a drink!

With the leak repaired, we were feeling happy and confident, believing that from now on all would be well. However, we were deluding ourselves as the problems mounted up, along with the frustrations. Here are more tales of our watery woes!

The exterior water main and stopcock serving our house and three others nearby is buried just over a metre deep. The key needed to turn off the water entering the properties is longer than the distance required to reach the tap, thereby providing enough room above ground to turn it using the large handle. Albert is responsible for looking after the key and is careful to leave it somewhere safe, but with easy access should residents need it. For some reason known only to installers and locals, the point of entry to the water main has nothing to identify its location. It seems the idea of a drain cover was never considered in that part of the world. Instead, trying to find it involves arming yourself with a shovel, taking a rough guess as to its location and then digging around for a couple of hours. If lucky, you will discover it, perhaps with a small slab of stone or piece of wood placed across the top of the access pipe, their purpose to prevent it filling with mud.

Our next leak meant summoning a new plumber, plumber number two; plumber number one being unavailable for some reason. We presumed he couldn't face a similar ordeal to the one experienced on his last visit. This new plumber managed to find the access point and using the key, attempted to turn off the water using the tap deep below the surface. It was stuck fast and struggles to loosen it resulted in the whole thing snapping off. The consequence of this meant that the copropriété had to delve into their coffers to pay for a small mechanical digger to excavate a large area right outside our door. The tap was duly accessed but was totally beyond help and deemed unrepairable.

This breakage caused all sorts of problems. The pipe that enters the house pops up vertically through the hall floor and makes a small ninety degree turn. It is impossible to empty when draining the pipes, as annoyingly, the interior stopcock is positioned several centimetres further along.

On arrival for another February stay, we tentatively switched on the water and within seconds, we were soaked, the dog was soaked and an indoor swimming pool was rapidly forming in the hallway. The joint between pipe and stopcock had frozen and split. Time to summon plumber number three; plumber number two had no doubt gone into hiding in case he faced a bill for the damage and resulting excavations from his last visit.

I felt sorry for plumber number three. To continue with the repair, he first needed to stop the water entering the house, which was, as you now know, impossible with the underground tap destroyed. His next course of action was to find the access point to the water main responsible for serving the whole of the *copropriété*. We simply had no idea where it was located, so consulted Albert who presented us with a hand drawn plan to study. Think treasure map; you know the sort of thing, five paces north, three paces to the east of the tree and 'X' marks the spot.

This plan described direction and rough distances, measured in metres, with a small fence post as the starting point. I clearly recall Albert, Rob and the plumber, standing around in the snow, in sub-zero temperatures, trying to find an 'X' that wasn't there. Shovels were acquired, snow scraped from a large area and attempts at digging made; this proved impossible as the soil was frozen solid. Next came a pickaxe which afforded some progress, but it was hard work and the poor plumber wasn't exactly built like a Marvel comic book hero. Nonetheless, he bravely fought on. Eventually, the access point was located. The possibilities for a drain cover at the time of construction, had once again been abandoned in favour of a more efficient method; a round stone and a tennis ball, both firmly lodged in the top of the access pipe. After removing these makeshift protectors, the plumber was able to use the special key to turn off the water without injury to himself or the tap. Rushing into the warmth of the house, he then replaced the joint before heading back out into the cold to restore the water to the properties. With the stone and tennis ball back in their rightful place inside the pipe, the snow and soil shovelled over, the access point was completely hidden, ensuring of course, we'd never be able to find it again.

Shortly after everyone had left, quick thinking Rob found a large boulder and plonked it on top, marking the position for future reference. It was a good job too, as the following year plumber number three was needed again to repeat the exact same process. This time he replaced the joint with a stronger one, but we knew the time had come to find a permanent solution.

We tried all sorts, from lagging and insulation to specially bought cables designed for use in vacant caravans, but nothing worked. Then Rob, who is an engineer, had a light bulb moment.

"I've been thinking", he said. "I've had an idea which might just work."

I have to admit, when he told me what it was, I was a little doubtful, but after a couple of trips to the DIY store for materials, he built his 'Heath Robinson' gizmo and set it up for testing. This new contraption worked a treat and has done so for years. It's also very cheap to run needing only one electrical switch left operating when we're not in residence. I think it's genius, (don't tell Rob I said that) and lots of family and friends agree. Well, as the saying goes, 'Necessity is the mother of invention.

Chapter 24
PEOPLE AND PIZZAS

Next door to Albert and Simone's, just beyond the bottom of their steps, sits a shelter. This is fondly referred to as the Pizza Hut. It is a cosy little place, well sheltered from the elements and contains a long table, with fixed and non-fixed bench seating, easily accommodating a dozen people. On one wall is a basin with running water and a small work surface with cupboards above. The back wall also has workspace, a built-in BBQ and best of all, a large, permanent, wood-fired pizza oven, complete with exterior thermometer. Although it's a shared resource for the *copropriété*, it is always thought of as belonging to Albert and Simone, probably because Albert built it.

Throughout our summers, we have eaten there often, enjoying the company of some lovely people, many of whom included Albert and Simone's extended family. Often the invitation would arrive via a shout through the window of the car as Albert and Simone passed by on the way to shop. Sometimes, if we were busy pottering outside, it might be shouted from their balcony. At other times it was delivered in person at our door or came via Gilbert and Annie, our neighbours, who also received an invite. We never refused and it became a regular event each year and one we very much looked forward to.

Sitting at the table with Gilbert and Annie, we'd watch Simone and Albert busy themselves preparing pizzas. Simone would make the dough and roll it out, Albert would be in charge of prepping the pizza oven, regularly checking the wood was burning well and ensuring the temperature was just right. Once the dough was ready, Albert, using the pizza shovel, skilfully placed the pizza base in the oven knowing exactly how long it would take to cook. Simone would then take the cooked base and smother it with Albert's homemade passata, finally adding her selected topping and sprinkling it with copious amounts of grated cheese. Another few minutes in the oven and it was ready.

We have never tasted pizza like it. Utterly perfect and what's more, they just kept on coming, each with a different topping and each shared around the six of us. On our very first visit, we stuffed our faces, struggling to down the last couple of mouthfuls, until all that remained were a few crumbs. Being the new kids on the block, we happily accepted the biggest slices each time, unaware there was more food to follow. By the time we'd nibbled our way through the large green salad, forced down some beautiful French cheeses that we had no room for and had our arms twisted, despite polite objections, to try *un peu de dessert*, we were at bursting point. Offering our thanks and refusing more wine, we took our leave and waddled back to the house, breathing a sigh of relief as we loosened our waistbands, knowing that next time, we'd be a whole lot wiser!

Although we lived next door to Gilbert and Annie, during our first couple of visits to the house, we only managed

Bonjour, conducting a polite conversation about how long we were staying and answering questions about our journey. These pizza evenings finally allowed us to get to know them a lot better.

Both been married before and had grown children. The circumstances around their marriage break-ups were never divulged, but it seemed they found happiness with each other and remained together ever since. To us, they seemed ideally matched. Both were ex-teachers, softly spoken and friendly. They were in their mid-fifties when we first met and learned that Gilbert's passions were cycling, hiking and running. His cycling was always a considerable distance, usually over steep inclines and his running involved routes up the side of a mountain. He was an incredibly fit guy and still is. Annie's hobbies, although she liked to go hiking occasionally, tended to be less energetic.

We knew from Annie that she had a daughter who lived in southwest France, but Gilbert never spoke about any children. It was Simone who revealed why. She explained that Gilbert had a son who'd lost his life under tragic circumstances. We were desperately sad to hear this. As it was obviously too painful for him to talk about, it would have been unseemly for us to pry, so we never did. We later learned that there were two grandsons which would have brought him a lot of comfort in the midst of the heartbreak. I know from personal experience that grandchildren help enormously in such circumstances. I lost my brother when he was just twenty-eight years old, a university graduate and geophysicist who would I'm sure, have been a force in the world had he lived. My parents were understandably devastated and totally heartbroken. Focusing their attentions on our very young children became a much needed distraction from the grief they were suffering. Over time, being grandparents helped them move forward from those dark days and into the light once more.

Gilbert and Annie were the perfect neighbours. They were kind, helpful and considerate. Gilbert would often ask during the summer months, if we had any objections to him using his tiny BBQ to prepare lunch, worrying the smoke might bother us. From time to time he would knock the door to warn us if any work he was carrying out inside his house might cause excess noise, such as hammering or drilling, hoping we wouldn't be disturbed. When we experienced our leaking pipe problems, he'd pop round with buckets full of water for us to use until the repair was completed. As with Simone and Albert, he and Annie's help and friendship have been invaluable across the years. Of course, we never ever objected to anything he requested and tried to be good neighbours in return.

On one occasion I remember, we thought we might have overstepped the mark. Max had picked up the scent of a bitch in heat. Love was definitely in the air judging from Max's warp speed as he careered through the commune. I sprinted after him arriving out of breath to witness our randy four-legged friend prowling back and forth gazing up at the object of his desire. The source of his lust turned out to be a sweet Cairn terrier, thankfully imprisoned behind a fence on a first floor balcony. She appeared to be as desperate as Max, whining longingly, returning his gaze while trying to clamber over the balcony railings. They were both out of luck, their lust was not about to be sated any time soon. I grabbed our amorous pet, attached his lead and was dragging a very reluctant Max back along the road when I passed by Gabriel. I greeted him cheerfully, asking how he was and after a cursory nod, he started to mumble something unintelligible about lights flashing and a *discothèque*. I had no idea what he appeared to be complaining about, but the fact he was nodding towards our balcony doors, I suspected we were the culprits. In appalling French, I muttered something about watching a film the previous evening and apologised if the volume had been a little excessive. I doubt he understood a word I'd said, except maybe the sorry bit.

Our TV was fixed on the wall near the balcony doors, which we believed could have been the source of the flickering lights he'd seen. As Rob had installed surround sound, the thump of the base on the soundtrack all added to Gabriel's perceptions of a *discothèque*. If he had picked up all this on the road below, we wondered whether Gilbert and Annie had been disturbed, even though we had no connecting wall. We immediately and somewhat guiltily popped round, knocked on their door and asked the question.

"*Pas de tout!*" Gilbert said "*Peut-être, occasionnellement, un petit bruit.*"

Being endlessly polite, Gilbert and Annie hearing an occasional small noise was obviously underplaying it, so Rob and I ensured volume and bass were lowered and blinds were fitted to the windows in our balcony doors. The next time we played a movie with a loud soundtrack, we stood outside for a little while with doors closed, listening carefully, double-checking we were not about to turn into a public nuisance and be the cause of indignant gossip.

August had rolled around again and Rosi and Jeff arrived for a week. We were especially thrilled because on this visit, they were accompanied by Dickie. Dickie was an artist we had met several years before on one our first visits to Key West when he would have been in his early sixties. He was a real character and a right old curmudgeon who didn't suffer the slightest twinge of guilt when being extremely rude to people who irritated him or whom he didn't like. He was a past master at delivering a cutting remark or the most withering of looks.   Anyone on the receiving end would be left in no doubt about how he felt, but underneath this scratchy exterior and sharp tongue, we knew he had a good heart and we just loved him.

He had great intellect and intelligence but was a real Luddite.   He refused to have anything to do with modern technology and wrote letters using an old typewriter.   We admired him for the great artist he was and, I suppose, for remaining true to himself, but he was a stubborn old sod too!

All three arrived in a hire car from Nice airport and Dickie spent his days standing in the shade, painting the fort or the ancient walls and entrances to the old town. He was now well into his seventies and hadn't driven for years but decided he was going to move himself around the area using the hire car, finding suitable locations to paint. With no obligation to drive him around, we were then free to please ourselves and go wherever we fancied.   Just one complication loomed that could scupper our plan; Dickie was a hopeless driver!   He never needed a car in Key West. The highest point is only 18 feet above sea level, the remainder of the small island being as flat as a pancake, so he happily used his trusty bicycle to get around, or scrounged a lift if he needed groceries or was going a little further out of town.

Jeff bravely accepted the job of testing Dickie's driving abilities, judging whether it was safe to let him loose on the mountain roads. The test would involve Dickie negotiating the car slowly down our narrow, steep little road to gauge how he fared. If all went well, he would then be allowed to head onto the main route into the village. He never made it as far as the main road. Arriving back at the house, Jeff got out of the car, now a nervous wreck, and pronounced Dickie unfit to drive after he'd scraped the car along a wall and nearly driven over the edge.

Dickie accepted this decision nobly; probably relieved he didn't have to struggle with a 'stick gear change" and hairpin bends. We hatched a plan to deliver him and his artist paraphernalia to his preferred spot in the village and dump him there for the day. He was perfectly happy with the arrangement and those in the local pâtisserie got to know him well as he popped in for his favourite cake every day.

Often he would find himself surrounded by people who were curious about his latest painting. He had no real French, so if they spoke to him he simply explained, "Je suis Américain," which seemed to satisfy his onlookers who would fall silent and eventually wander off. If a couple of folk began to irritate him by getting too close, peering at his canvas over his shoulder and spoiling his concentration, he would give them the full benefit of his withering stare and acid tongue.

"What the bloody hell are you looking at? Nothing better to do than hang around me all day? Bugger off!"

I doubt they understood what he was saying, but the meaning was clear enough and they would scarper pretty sharpish.

After a day's outing, we'd collect Dickie at the agreed time and return home to settle down with a pre-dinner drink. Dickie never diversified away from his favourite cocktail, a healthy measure of vodka, with a splash of tonic and a tiny sliver of lemon peel. Our evenings, when conversation was exhausted, would be spent occasionally playing Scrabble, which he loved, or watching favourite videos. He was almost unbeatable at Scrabble, having a huge lexicon of words in his head that he used to great effect, several of which we'd never heard of! Throughout his week with us, he produced at least a dozen small, superb canvasses and before he left, he let us choose one as a gift for looking after him. The following year, on a holiday to Key West, he'd had it framed and carefully wrapped for us to bring home.

Chapter 25
A PROBLEM WITH SATELLITES

Although being occupied most of the time with walking, exploring, skiing or participating in the simple enjoyment of lazing about outside on a summer's evening, sipping a nice glass of vino and watching the sun go down, we did need entertainment inside the house for those cold winter nights and rainy days. We had a stack of board games and read a lot, but music and TV were also essential. The first two years we managed with a small portable TV, watching limited French channels, all of which were dreadful, seemingly swamped by quiz programs and adverts. To see the TV screen, you needed binoculars or had to sit within an arm's length peering at it, the fuzzy picture making you squint until you began to see double. It was a rare event we ever switched the thing on.

Back then, we were more thrilled with our multi CD player; never ones to miss out on the latest gadgets! At least we could listen to our favourite music while curled up with a good book. Since then, we've tweaked and upgraded as technology demanded; currently, we are totally miffed that our iPod is now considered a relic of a bygone age, a bit like us I suppose, a little out of date, but still useful ... but I digress. With a new flat screen TV in place, we took the decision to buy and set up a satellite system.

I never attempt anything without doing copious amounts of research and I became reasonably informed on satellites, azimuths, LNBs and skew alignment. Our first dish installation took place with me as acting supervisor, supplying instructions to a resentful Rob balanced on a ladder, who insisted he knew what he was doing, thank you! Our joint efforts were not wholly successful. It did work but failed to pick up UK TV in bad weather and in good weather the picture remained pixelated. For some reason, during the summer months, it didn't work at all. It was back to the drawing board.

Once home, with my head buried in the internet again, reading lots of 'blokey' type blogs. I discovered that UK TV channels were transmitted via satellites called Astra 2 or Eurobird. We needed Astra 2, but UK TV channels move as upgraded Astra 2 satellites come on stream. It seemed the BBC had received complaints from many living in the extreme north of Scotland. The residents, a little peed off at having to pay a licence fee to receive a dismal signal, or none at all, bombarded the BBC with complaints. To keep the Scots happy, the BBC jumped ship to an upgraded Astra 2 and narrowed the beam, focussing it on the entire UK thereby abandoning most of France and Spain. Other UK channels did much the same.

I then gleaned from reading all this technical stuff, that it might just be possible to pick up signals in this corner of France, even half-way up a mountain, but we'd need a larger dish to catch them. Some internet sites recommended a dish so big that we'd have been giving Goonhilly Downs a run for its money, so after consulting with our French mate Bob, we bought a dish in France which came with two LNBs, you know, those things that sit in the middle of the dish for picking up the signal. Admittedly, it was a tad larger than our old one, but not so big that it was in danger of casting a shadow over the whole commune and bringing down the wall of our house.

This was where the fun began and we were grateful Ben was there to help. The ten pages of information I had printed off at home were ignored as Rob and son struggled to find a signal. Discarding compasses and degrees of azimuth, both of which were complete failures, they decided to follow the simple advice, that of pointing the LNBs to just under the position of the sun at 11 o'clock in the morning and avoiding any obstructions which could block the signal. This is fine if the sun is shining; or if the tree located near the house isn't there; or if a couple of mountains could be dumped elsewhere. None of this being possible, it was down to guesswork and luck. The satellite dish was moved hither and thither in the hope of locating that magic signal. At one point with it attached to a long wooden pole, Rob and Ben slowly paraded up and down the balcony like some weird demonstration march, manoeuvring the dish in all directions. Failing miserably, Ben then risked life and limb clambering onto the roof of the house with it, hoping the extra six metres of elevation might help. It didn't. The wall outside the balcony doors also became the victim of several holes, drilled in varying positions where the dish had been mounted and then promptly dismounted as it failed to work. Nikki and I, in the meantime, had to spend hours looking at a TV screen waiting for something to happen on the signal power readout, yelling periodically if a sniff of one appeared, then shouting again when it disappeared a few seconds later.

"Think you're getting a signal! Move it a bit. Noooo! Wrong direction, signal's gone! Try moving it the other way. No, nothing! Why not try the roof!"

Nothing worked, and so the saga continued. This whole

palaver went on for two days before we achieved success and the dish finally installed just outside the balcony doors, about a couple metres above the deck. Nikki and I had found the whole thing highly amusing, as watching Rob and Ben moving this dish all over the place was quite funny. They, on the other hand, didn't see the funny side at all. I can just hear you all saying, why not get a trained satellite installer to do it? Just try finding one! It seems they're as rare as hen's teeth in our little part of the world, preferring to live hundreds of miles away in some large city where demand is plentiful.

At last, the numerous unneeded holes in the wall were filled and any cables tidied away neatly. Now we could sit back, relax, watch the news from home and catch up on a favourite TV programme, or so we thought. Nothing is ever that easy. Switching on and faced with over 1,000 listed TV channels, many from places we'd never heard of, it was going to take yet another day to sort it all out. We gave a collective groan ...

"Anyone up for a Taiwanese soap opera then?"

Chapter 26
WHEN THE CHIMNEY SWEEPS CAME CALLING

Our log fire is one of the joys of being at the house in autumn and winter. It's the sheer delight of hunkering down in its warmth and spending a moment watching the flames dance, hearing the comforting spit and crackle as it consumes the logs then letting your eyes stray, following the fall of fat snowflakes as they float past the window. My love of the snow will usually encourage a swift expedition to the end of the balcony accompanied by Max , who as you know, adores the snow as much as I do. Poking a toe outside reminds me just how cold it is and a quick forage into the white stuff is all I need before my toes start turning blue, not helped by the fact I'm usually in my slippers. Max and I tumble into the house, dragging snow with us. Rob refrains from this childish behaviour.

"Shut the door! You're letting all the heat out!" he shouts, at the same time, moving rapidly out of the way as Max shakes the cold remnants of snow from his hairy coat, straight in Rob's direction.

As children in our council-owned properties, we have

abiding memories of coal fires, and soot-covered coalmen who delivered heavy black sacks of the stuff which they hoisted down the garden path on their shoulders and deposited it in what we referred to as the coal hole. This wasn't the proper name, it not being a hole, but a large cupboard space with planks across to stop the coal from falling out. It also had a door. It was dark and smelly and I swear, full of spiders, and you know what I think of them! I determined this because my brother used to lock me in it on a regular basis when my parents went out. I still recall sitting on top of the coal, screaming my head off until released. When 'real' fires disappeared as coal was eventually ruled out by the Clean Air Act, like everyone, we became accustomed to the luxury of living with central heating, but there is still nothing like a real fire and the smell of burning wood to make you feel cosy and safe.

Our French house is equipped with central heating, which if kept on for long periods of time, is likely to result in bankruptcy. Hence the fact that everyone in the mountains tends to burn wood and in the case of Gabriel and Marcella, anything flammable they can lay their hands on. We have long wondered exactly what they put on their fire as the smoke from their chimney is enough to poison the entire community and beyond. Black smoke, thick enough to cut into chunks, swirls out into the air and drifts happily in our direction. Washing needs to be retrieved rapidly before becoming dirtier than it was to start with and a frustrated Max, in need of a *pi-pi* is forbidden to venture out until the evil smelling smoke dissipates. Thankfully, this doesn't last more than ten minutes before you can head outside without breathing apparatus. We loved our big log fire, and have always been careful to only burn suitable wood, but apart from ensuring we had enough logs and cleaning the fire thoroughly after use, our minds didn't stretch to chimney sweeps, so it came as a bit of surprise when they came knocking one day.

They arrived in summer, one morning in early August. The weather was perfect; a cloudless blue sky with hardly any breeze. The rays of the sun were just hitting the Fort de Savoie at the foot of the valley while the mountain tops were already basking in the heat. I was still swanning about in my nightie and Rob was in his underpants. We heard a knock and someone entering the outer hall shouting *"Bonjour, bonjour!"* I made a dash up the stairs to protect my modesty and Rob grabbed and put on the shorts he'd dumped on the sofa the night before. Max made a feeble attempt at barking. With my modesty restored, I came down to be greeted by two individuals, one of whom was male, very small in stature and covered in soot. Surely they didn't still send people up chimneys, I thought as I stared at this little man. He was certainly small enough to try. The woman with him, who turned out to be his wife, was taller, but still relatively short and a great deal sturdier than her spouse, with lots of muscle and little fat. She explained they were here to clean the chimney. She said they did so every year and it was imperative because we needed a signed document to prove it had been done. The cost was reasonable enough, but we explained we had only had one week's worth of fires this year back in February, so the job did seem a little unnecessary. However, this was one determined lady, who gave Rob the full force of her blue-eyed gaze.

"*Pfft*! *mais Chef*, what will you do if your house burns down? Your insurance, it will not work without the document."

I must point out at this juncture that she was not crediting Rob with any kind of culinary flair, but was firmly placing him as head honcho in our household, as well as using flattery and a bit of flirting to ensure she would secure the job!

We relented, not because of her attention to Rob's supposed seniority and possible attraction where female chimney sweeps were concerned, but because we had visions of becoming destitute if the house burned down along with any chance of remuneration.   A few moments later her *petit* husband was busy moving furniture and ornaments to safety before settling into his task of sucking up any remnants of ash from the fireplace with his specialist vacuum. We were glad to see he was not attempting to shimmy up the chimney. By now, his wife had disappeared. A shout outside, a tiny fall of soot and a brush head appeared in the fireplace.

"Blimey," said Rob, "She must be on the roof."

To prove him wrong, I went outside to check and sure enough, there she was, negotiating herself around the roof *sans peur*, totally fearless of the massive drop on the south side of the roof.

Less than twenty minutes later, she was back on solid ground, her small spouse was back in the driving seat of their van, just visible behind the steering wheel, money was paid and a signed certificate issued.

"*A bientôt. L'année prochaine!*" she shouted as their van disappeared in a cloud of dust back down the track.

"Well that was surprise," I said after this unexpected visit. "I reckon she fancies you," I teased.

Rob looked at me with disdain. "Yeah, right. Can you imagine? I'd never get out of her grip if she got hold of me. Doesn't bear thinking about," said Rob with a shudder. "Mind you, she'd be useful doing all the heavy jobs around the house," he said pretending to look thoughtful.

Laughing, I looked him in the eye and said "Just think, a whole year before she's here again, and you know what they say, 'absence makes the heart grow fonder'."

True to her word, they came the following year and have continued to do so. Madame chimney sweep has the looks of a gypsy. She has short, jet black hair and the sort of weathered complexion you get from working outside all year. She also has perfectly white teeth, a rarity in France, as most of the teeth we've seen show an alarming lack of dentistry. She has startling blue eyes and yes, Madame chimney sweep is a bit scary. I certainly wouldn't have wanted to get on the wrong side of her, though I suspect Rob could have got away with it. Definitely built for strength, I could see why Rob acknowledged she would scare the life out of him if it came to it. I was also certain she inherited some psychic gene from her possible Romany heritage, often wondering how they both knew we were in residence as they never missed a beat and turned up regardless of the month or week. If we had visitors occupying the house in our absence, Monsieur and Madame chimney sweep never made an appearance. They just spirited themselves up once we were back again.

August had rolled around and we were back again enjoying our little French bolthole. It was a gorgeous sunny morning in the mountains. At the sound of a van approaching, I suspected our chimney sweeps were about to make their annual visit.

From conversations with Albert and Simone, we discovered the chimney sweeps lived in Manosque and came to the area every year, touring around the villages and communes plying their trade. Arriving around the beginning of July, they remained until the end of August when most people had left their holiday homes to return to work. We often said that cleaning chimneys must be a lucrative business as their Renault van was large, reasonably new and had their details and occupation professionally painted on both sides. While going about their business, they stayed comfortably in their large motorhome in one of the 'camping car' spaces in the village. We have no idea whether they continued their trade elsewhere or had other jobs to tide them over once summer was a distant memory.

On this visit, their grown son, decidedly taller than both parents, with the same swarthy looks as his mother but lacking her personality, had now joined the family business. On this occasion, Madame chimney sweep didn't come along and the duties fell to her miniscule husband and tall son. This might have been a relief for Rob, but I still acquired a load of ammunition to tease him with when one day, while reversing out of a parking space in the village, she walked across in front of us. She looked directly at me. The French always look at the passenger side first, the side they expect to see the driver. I received a cursory glance. She obviously didn't recognise me and failed to respond, even though I smiled at her. She then noticed Rob, stopped dead, delivered a huge smile and little wave before moving off keeping her eyes glued to him until she was out of sight.

"Told you," I said to Rob, "You'd better make sure you're not alone in the house next time she arrives. Could prove to be dangerous."

Rob gave me a playful slap on the arm and boasted, "Well, you know women can't resist my charm and youthful looks."

"Yeah, right," I said, eyeing his greying hair and gently patting his expanding waistline.

Chapter 27
THE LITTLE RESTAURANT

From my previous ramblings, you will recall there was a tiny restaurant at the bottom of the road that leads up to our commune. This road is narrow and very steep, which ensured however full we were feeling after enjoying a meal in this little venue, we were sure to have walked it off by the time we arrived back at the house. It was named the Eau Vive, meaning 'living water' due to its proximity to a small river that tumbled over rocks and stones on its descent into the Verdon.

The restaurant, located in a small, single storey building, was attached to a little two-storey house. Whether or not the owners of the house owned the restaurant building, we've never found out. Inside were four neat rows of tables, one of which lay directly against the windows that ran the length of the building, overlooking the rushing waters of the river below. Sadly, outside dining space was impossible due to the restaurant walls sitting right on the edge of the steep river bank.

We ate at the Eau Vive several times enjoying the conviviality of the place. The food was typical fare for the region, reasonably priced and tasted good. Passing by one day, heading to the house for another joyous escape from the world of work, we noticed it had closed down. With further investigation needed, our first point of enquiry was naturally Simone. She told us the restaurateurs had left and moved to pastures new, explaining they didn't get enough business to survive and were losing money.

We were horribly disappointed to have lost our cosy little restaurant. It always appeared busy whenever we visited, but whatever the cause, we would just have to survive without it and comforted ourselves knowing there were other restaurants to frequent in the villages along the valley. Later that year, back in residence once again, we bumped into Richard who informed us, much to our delight, that our little restaurant was re-opening. One of his friends, he said, was moving into the valley and taking over the business.

Richard was most enthusiastic, saying, "You must come, my English friends. Alain and Marie are *très agréable*, very nice, and the food is *très bon*. We must go to help it, how you say, have success. See you soon, yes?"

We were very happy to oblige and it wasn't long before we headed down for a meal. Richard had introduced us to the new proprietors. Friendly and welcoming, we took to them immediately. The food was great too; simple fare cooked well. Marie knew I loved *fromage blanc*, drizzled with raspberry coulis and would pre-empt my request by writing it down on her notepad before I said anything. Because of our association with Richard, they treated us like friends and would always try to spend a few minutes chatting if they were not too busy.

We visited many times with friends and relatives who came to stay and would often bump into Michel and Sylvanna and their family or Richard out with his mates. It was especially nice to go down in autumn and winter when it was dark and cold outside, knowing that within its walls it was warm and cosy as the log burner worked its magic.

On one such cold autumn evening, Albert and Simone asked if we wanted to attend a special *Grand Aioli* event they'd seen advertised at the restaurant. We had no idea what a *Grand Aioli* was, but they came to the rescue by explaining it was a rustic Provençal dish made with meat and vegetables and served with *aioli*. It sounded fine to us. We have always liked *aioli* as we're fans of the tasty *soupe de poisson*, so famous in the south, usually accompanied by this pungent, garlicky, mayonnaise-type sauce spread generously on crunchy, toasted baguette slices or croutons and dropped on top.

We settled at our table, basking in the warmth after the chilly walk down; Albert and Simone had driven. The *Grand Aioli* arrived in a dish so large it was big enough to bath a baby in, and barely left room for anything else at the table. A second, smaller dish containing the most *aioli* I've seen in one place was delicately squeezed in.

"Is that for everyone in the restaurant?" I asked. "I've never seen so much meat and veg."

"I know," said Rob. "And the meat is in huge pieces. Look," he said, delving into the dish and indicating what looked like a whole ham, huge chunks of lamb and lots more besides.

I kid you not. It was definitely a carnivore's dream.

Vegetarians didn't miss out, though most of the vegetables provided were of the root variety, full sized and whole, the carrots still in possession of their green tops. The idea was to grab your chosen vegetable and scoop up a hefty amount of *aioli*, then spend the next ten minutes trying to nibble through it. Albert and Simone were not joking when they said it was rustic.

Rob and I ploughed through as much as we could, but once we had eaten enough to feed a small army and could barely move, it still looked like we'd hardly touched it. Needless to say, we refused pudding!

Since that night, we have come across this kind of meal often, usually listed on a menu board as simply *Aioli,* with each restaurant having its own take on what it should be. More often than not, the offering is a more refined version, a lot smaller in both content and amount that always proves popular with diners. I usually order something else!

Under its new stewardship, the Eau Vive was flourishing with hardly a seat available at lunchtime or during the evenings whenever we ventured down. Therefore, it was with some shock, just over eighteen months later, it closed suddenly. Once again, Rob and I sought out Albert and Simone to 'dish the dirt' on why this had happened for the second time. Simone got into her stride,

"Alors! C'est un catastrophe!" Then, lowering her voice for dramatic effect, *"Les propriétaires, ils ont disparu dans las nuit."*

It appeared that Alain and Marie had done a midnight flit leaving behind a lot of debt. No one knew where they'd gone. Richard denied all knowledge of their whereabouts, shrugging his shoulders in response to our enquiry. Whether or not they took off with the takings without paying their bills, or whether the business genuinely fell into debt and they fled to avoid financial ruin, we'll never know. It proved to be sensational gossip for a while in our little corner of the world. We were just sad to see our lovely little restaurant empty and abandoned once more.

BACK AND FORTH

We have spent many years hurtling down the *Autoroute* to reach the house and have thankfully avoided any accidents, though early on we had a very lucky escape. Travelling towards Sisteron, in terrible weather, the car started to skid badly, swerving from side to side, almost ending in a full spin. We had hit surface water and the car aquaplaned. I was so grateful I'd bought Rob a rally-driving day for his birthday several years previously, and that he'd also completed an advanced driving test, as it meant he had the skills to control the skid. We avoided crashing into the central barrier and with no-one alongside us, escaped serious injury to others and ourselves. Someone was obviously looking out for us that day. I have no idea how I remained calm while Rob was bringing the car under control, but I do remember feeling very queasy once the emergency was over, nearly throwing up in the footwell!

Having a house in France has allowed us to explore new areas and to re-visit others we really liked. Our explorations usually happen on the homeward journey back to the UK when we take the opportunity to divert somewhere interesting for a short nose around or spend longer if the area is new to us. As I'm not writing a travelogue, I won't ramble on about the places we've been to, but funny things can happen. Here are a couple that we experienced

Chapter 28
THE CHATEAU

One thing we had not done since buying our little French house was to visit Peter Mayle's Provence, the area that inspired us to start our own French house-buying adventure. It was also the area in which we now found ourselves, sitting in a farmyard not far from the village of Valreas.

Valreas is famous for its red wine that is often quite expensive, so wanting to grab the chance to buy some from an actual *vigneron* (wine grower) was an opportunity not to be missed. We spied a hand-painted notice at the side of the road announcing *dégustation gratuite*. Helpfully, an arrow pointed us in the right direction and we were soon enjoying a bone-shaking journey along a dirt track pitted with potholes and large rocks. I was convinced something would be shaken loose, such as car parts and our teeth, but the promise of free wine tasting was too hard to resist.

We eventually came to a farmyard and in seconds the car was surrounded by a pack of barking dogs hurling themselves at the doors.

"I am not getting out with that lot around." I said with trepidation, eyeing the pack through the window.

"Oh for heaven's sake," resassured Rob. "You love dogs. They'll be fine."

"I know I love dogs, thank you, but not a whole pack of vicious looking guard dogs who could rip your throat open in minutes. Why don't you get out then?" I asked Rob who was now looking a tad reluctant to move. "Besides, where is everyone? The place is as quiet as the grave!"

As soon as the words were out of my mouth, the dogs stopped their barking as one of the tallest men I've ever seen appeared, shouting at the dogs to calm down and giving us a huge grin as he approached the car.

Feeling a whole lot braver now the dogs were under control, we finally left the safety of the car to find ourselves surrounded by at least eight canines of varying sizes, tails wagging furiously, all vying for our attention. The fear of attack now gone, Rob and I were busy making acquaintance with our new four-legged friends while the seven-foot giant was shaking our hands in turn, asking, *"Bonjour! Es-tu venu pour goûter du vin?"* We replied in the affirmative. The giant then explained that he wasn't in charge of the tasting, but he'd fetch his mother to organise it for us.

He and the dogs disappeared through the farmhouse door, and a few minutes later, a tiny woman emerged. She must have been under five feet tall and as Rob and I followed her into a large barn, we wondered how this little lady had managed to produce such a huge son.

"Blimey, I uttered, I bet he was an enormous baby. Can you imagine? The thought of it is making my eyes water!"

We spent the next half an hour sampling some beautiful wines served in paper cups full to the brim! Rob, who was driving, kept secretly passing his cup to me after tasting a small amount, asking me to finish it so we didn't appear rude. I looked desperately for somewhere to dispose of the excess wine, but other than form a large puddle on the floor, giving the game away, I had no choice but to drink it. The result of glugging copious amounts of wine in a relatively short span of time had the expected results. I began to feel decidedly squiffy!

With wine purchased, we headed off after asking our little lady *vigneron* if she knew somewhere we could stay that night. She recommended a *château* a few miles further north.

Château Number 1

Half an hour later, as we were entering through the huge ornate gates, Rob turned to me, "No way can we stop here," he said. "Just look at that lot!" He was referring to the guests' cars, the type of which would not be out of place in a James Bond movie or a Premier League player's car park.

"Don't be daft, they're no better than us!" I slurred as I stumbled out of the car and strode into the very impressive Reception area with Rob following behind. The receptionist gave us a disdainful examination, me swaying happily in Rob's wake as he approached the desk. His enquiry about a room was met with a fixed smile as she looked from him to me and back again. "*Non, Monsieur 'Dame*. We 'ave no rooms, only the bridal suite is vacant," she responded, haughtily.

"The snotty cow!" I drunkenly thought. "Who the hell does she think she's talking to! Not good enough? I'll show her!" I leaned carefully on the desk to deliver my *coup de grâce*. "That will be splendid, won't it dahling," I slurred in the poshest voice I could muster.

Miss Snotty-pants looked startled and Rob looked as though he was going to faint. He rapidly recovered in time to save the day and prevent our imminent bankruptcy, "I'm sorry, I'm sure the bridal suite will be far too big for us for just one night. Can you recommend anywhere that might have a double room vacant?"

To be fair, she recommended one of the nicest places

we've ever stayed.

Château Number 2

Further north still, we arrived at a lovely little château situated in a beautiful spot, just outside Montelimar. Heading through the small entrance, we were greeted warmly by the two male owners who were squeezed behind the tiny reception desk in the corner. *"Bonjour, bonjour! Bienvenue! Welcome to our 'otel. I am Pierre, zis eez my partner Maurice and zis is Verity"* he said, indicating the white Cairn Terrier lying across the reception desk. Rubbing her behind the ears and making little cooing sounds, Maurice continued, *"She eez our petite princesse. She eez very especial,"* he gushed while planting a series of little kisses on her head. *"She eez Engleesh",* he continued with pride in his voice. *"We travel to Angleterre to get 'er. We buy ze best. She is very beautiful, n'est-ce pas?*

We agreed she was indeed very pretty and said it was nice to have a dog in residence as we had just lost our dog Roxy.

"Oh, zat is SO triste!" We would die if anysink should 'appen to our princesse!" said Pierre, grabbing onto Verity as though she was about to keel over there and then. After reassuring himself and Maurice that nothing terrible was about to happen, he finally dragged himself away from their little pooch and showed us to our stunning room. We were so impressed, we immediately asked him if we could stay for two nights and thankfully, he granted our request.

The following day, after enjoying a beautifully presented buffet breakfast, we headed off to explore the delights of Montelimar. We wandered up and down its narrow streets peering in shop windows filled with *nougat,* the confection Montelimar is famous for, colourfully displayed in every imaginable flavour and in a variety of shapes and sizes. We had never seen so much, and couldn't resist buying some exquisitely wrapped samples to take back to the UK as presents.

It was a fabulous day weather-wise and feeling rather sticky in the heat, we eventually headed back to the *château* to enjoy the delights of their outdoor pool. It was pure bliss swimming in the full sized pool. Besides being deliciously cool, it afforded great views from its vantage point overlooking the surrounding countryside. Comfortably perched on top of the slope behind us, lay the little *château*, looking like something out of a fairy tale with its pale stone walls reflecting the sunlight and two rounded towers pointing towards the blue sky. We both agreed it was a very special place to stay.

That evening we headed out onto the terrace where the tables were beautifully laid in readiness for dinner. A little early, we settled ourselves away from the terrace in a swing seat. Gently swaying back and forth, slowly sipping our *aperitifs,* we gazed at the stars in the night sky. It was so peaceful with just the quiet murmur of conversation floating on the air as diners began to congregate. Then all hell broke loose.

Earlier in the day, we had noticed a dog confidently trotting around the local village as if he owned it. Of indeterminate breed with a sandy coloured coat, long thin tail and wiry build, he looked every inch the local ne'er-do-well. What made him even more roguish was the fact he was missing an eye which obviously didn't bother this cocky character one bit, and there he was now, right in the midst of the commotion which had caused the diners to temporarily abandon their meals to see what was going on.

From our swing seat, we had a birds-eye view as the large, round figure of the chef launched himself out of the doorway that led from the kitchen, waving his arms and yelling at the top of his voice,

"Merde, merde! Non, non NON! Arrête ça! Arrête ça maintenant!"

At first, we couldn't see what he was so desperate to stop, but all became clear when a bucket of water was quickly produced and thrown over the prized Verity and the one-eyed rogue from the village, both of whom had been busily engaged in the act of copulation. The 4-legged Casanova had put a lot of vigorous effort into his love-making and Verity had definitely enjoyed herself.

"Oh God, that's hilarious," Rob sniggered. "Just wait until Maurice and Pierre find out their little princess has been having some fun with the village ruffian."

"It's like a canine version of Lady Chatterley's lover." I responded.

The water had the desired effect and stopped all activity in an instant. Stuck end to end, as is the case with post-coitus dogs, the villain of the piece was unable to escape for a while. Eventually he extricated himself from his royal lover, and before he hightailed it over the stone wall in search of another conquest, he turned his one good eye towards the viewing public and I swear he winked!

It wasn't long before Maurice and Pierre rushed out of the kitchen and scooped up their bedraggled pooch,

"Oh Verity, Verity, notre princesse, notre bébé", they cooed. *"Mon Dieu, c'est un catastrophe!"*

She didn't look the least bit bothered at having been rogered by the local canine lothario, but probably did object to the injection she had to have at the vets the next day.

Eventually, peace returned. The diners had stopped laughing and returned to their meals. Rob and I joined them on the terrace, still tittering over what we'd just witnessed.

We did wonder if that cheeky four-legged character ever got a second chance at making Verity the mother of his children. We never did find out because when we returned a couple of years later, we found the *château* gates chained and a notice explaining that the *château* had closed. From enquiries made at a nearby hotel, it seems that Maurice and Pierre had struggled financially and eventually had no choice but to leave. We were very sad to hear this as they were perfect hosts and went to a lot of trouble to make their guests feel welcome. We often wonder where they are now and very much hope they managed to find success elsewhere.

Chapter 29
MAXWELL'S DISGUSTING HABIT

Why do dogs roll in poo? We had cause to ask this question countless times. Max was masterful at it, highly skilled at locating and ensuring maximum coverage of the most evil-smelling, slimy, disgusting deposits he could find. He also put on an Oscar-winning performance of total joy and conceit as he strutted around, thoroughly coated, showing everyone just how clever he was, all the time knowing this activity met with deep disapproval from Rob and myself.

For some reason, France seemed to be the most marvellous location for poo spotting - from a dog's perspective I hasten to add. Rob and I certainly don't spend our time creeping around trying to spy the stuff. We also questioned why many deposits seemed to be left by *Homo sapiens*, usually behind trees or hidden in bushes. You are probably wondering how we know this. After all, it's more likely to belong to a woodland creature of some sort. Well, woodland creatures, as far as we're aware, do not use toilet paper.

One occasion that particularly sticks in my mind was when we were heading back to the tunnel from a week's stay at the house. We had decided to take a short diversion in order to visit the source of the Seine. A sign in front of a small grotto containing a tiny pool of water declared that Napoleon had decided this was the spot! It wasn't very impressive, but Max was having fun getting his feet muddy in the miniscule trickle of water emanating from the grotto and enjoying the opportunity to hare around a large open area after being cooped up in his cage for hours.

It was autumn, the skies were leaden, it was chilly, it was damp and the place was utterly deserted. Being in the middle of nowhere, I can understand the reluctance of anyone wanting to visit on such a dreary day. After spending a couple of minutes gazing at Napoleon's discovery, we needed to get our blood moving before the chill reached our bones. Standing around staring at a puddle wasn't exactly enthralling either, so the three of us followed a small footpath which took us in a circular route around the perimeter of the park.

I had arrived back at the start and turned to see Rob, lingering behind, calling Max who had disappeared behind a large oak tree. As a well-trained pooch, Max emerged and Rob screeched, jumping backwards with admirable dexterity. At this point, I should mention that Rob is a complete wimp when it comes to unpleasant smells and usually begs me to come to the rescue as he either (i) runs away, or (ii) starts heaving! In this instance, he didn't run away, but shouted at the top of his voice.

"Nooooo! Max! OMG, he's rolled. God it's bloody awful! He's absolutely plastered in it. Jesus! It's human! God, he smells revolting!!

Rob was now rapidly backing away from the dog. Max eyed him carefully and chose to follow, thinking this might prove to be an interesting game.

"Do something!" Rob cried, as Max stood next to him, tail

wagging, wafting a cloud of nauseating aroma up Rob's nostrils.

"For God's sake!" I shouted. "Lead him down here and we'll have to see if we can clean him up. There's no way he's going in the car smelling like that!"

"Well don't expect *me* to touch him!" Rob stated firmly, finally arriving at my side with our slimy, brown, hideously smelly dog following behind. I needed to think of a solution...

"Right," I said to Rob. "You've got to be brave. If you can grab his front and back legs and upend him in that miniscule stream, you could swoosh him back and forth to get the worst of it off!"

Rob looked at me in disbelief.

"What? Are you mad? I can't do it. You know what I'm like with smells."

"Oh, stop being a wimp and get on with it, unless you're ok with sharing the car with Max and breathing in that smell ALL the way home."

If looks could kill, I'd be dead and buried, but after a bit of egging on and excuses from me about how I wasn't strong enough to carry out the task, Rob bravely ventured towards our mucky pet and attempted to do what I'd suggested.

Have you ever tried to upend a reluctant dog by simply holding front paws in one hand and the back paws in the other? It doesn't work. Max was highly indignant about such treatment and struggled back onto his feet. Rob meanwhile was standing away, as far as possible from the smelly creature while trying not to release his grip on him.

It was at this point that Max decided to shake himself. Rob hung on, hoping to prevent what was about to happen and started yelling like a banshee for Max to stop. Max doesn't understand the command 'Stop.' I had legged it to a safe distance as Max divested himself of a large amount of the brown stuff that was now flying through the air in a cloud of pungent drops, with Rob directly in the firing line.

"No! ... No, Max!! Stop ... STOP! Oh, my God!! Oh, no, I've got the stuff on my face! I think I can taste it!" Yelled Rob.

Spying me standing at a safe distance, bent double with mirth, being no help whatsoever, he ranted, "What the hell are you laughing at! You knew this would happen! It's not bloody funny!"

"Oh, it is, it really is," I muttered, tears running down my face.

With Max eyeing us suspiciously from a safe distance, I finally brought myself under some kind of control. Rob had now stopped his rant and I had formulated a plan. Ten minutes later, using the entire contents of a large bottle of drinking water, some shower gel retrieved from our luggage and a towel, we loaded a clean, beautifully smelling Max back into the car. Rob, too, was now devoid of any evidence of Max's activity after cleaning himself up and changing his top.

As we pulled away from the scene of this debacle, feeling pleased with myself I smugly stated, "Glad I thought of that even if it was me who had to clean him up as always. Max smells as fresh as a daisy now."

"Yes, but it's a pity you didn't come up with that idea FIRST and did you have to use the ENTIRE bottle of my VERY expensive shower gel?" moaned Rob. "Do you know how much that stuff costs?"

Five minutes later, with the image of Rob and Max replaying like a film in my head ....

"Haven't you stopped sniggering yet?" asked Rob. "It wasn't THAT funny!"

"Oh it was ... it definitely was." I said.

Chapter 30
BRINGING THINGS UP TO DATE

We have never regretted purchasing our little French house and love it as much now as we always did. It is such a joy to arrive and open the shutters, never tiring of the view down the valley from the balcony. Our one regret has been that none of our parents ever managed to see it.

My parents had passed away before we bought it, though I always say, 'I carry them in my pocket' and when I'm on the balcony basking in the view, I can often imagine my lovely dad standing next to me, saying, "Very nice J, very nice." My dad was never one to enthuse too wildly, but I know he'd have liked it and been very proud of us too. My mum would have loved it. She liked great scenery, along with peace and quiet, but as she always described herself as a homing pigeon, she wouldn't have wanted to stay for long before yearning to return to familiar territory.

My lovely parents-in-law never got there, eventually becoming too frail to manage the terrain around the house. I will never forget visiting my father-in-law while he was in hospital, seemingly regaining strength after a serious illness.

He was now a widower, having lost my mum-in-law to dementia. As Rob and I were taking our leave, he shouted across the ward, "When I get out of here, I'm definitely coming to that French house of yours!" I gave him the thumbs up and told him, "Absolutely!" That was the last time we saw him as he passed away unexpectedly a week later.

Life continues in the valley with people coming and going, new chalets springing up, roads improved and the ski resort investing in new lift systems. Nothing stands still for long.

So, before you go, let me bring you right up to date with what has been happening to the people and places in our little corner of France that you've come to know.

Albert and Simone

We had to say goodbye to these lovely people as they were forced to permanently move back to their home in Saint Tropez. They were both getting too frail to cope, especially in the wintertime. They hated leaving, but Albert was beginning to find it hard to move around safely. He had already been fitted with a heart pacemaker and his balance wasn't what it was. Simone, who did all the driving, was also finding life difficult. She'd had a couple of operations to insert stents into the arteries of her heart, and although these were entirely successful, regular check-ups required her to travel back and forth from the mountains to St Tropez on a regular basis which was proving too much.

Back in St Tropez, now both well into their 90s, Albert's health deteriorated after having his leg amputated below the knee because of bad circulation. Simone was as stubborn as ever and apparently refused any outside help, preferring to look after her husband herself. We very much missed our wonderful French 'mum and dad' who had looked out for us over so many years and were utterly heartbroken when Gilbert emailed to say that Albert had passed away in early November

2019. He was such a wonderful human being who will always hold a special place in our hearts. It was a privilege to have known him.

Their little house will eventually pass to members of their extended family who still use it from time to time, but sadly, the pizza hut where we've spent so many memorable evenings, had fallen into disrepair. On a recent visit, we discussed with Gilbert the possibility of restoring it, the perfect way to honour the memory of the man who built it. He agreed and we're hoping the rest of the *copropriété* will acquiesce and consent to release a small amount of funding to pay for materials. I also think we should name it *Albert's*.

Gabriel and Marcella

Gabriel lived well into his 90s and passed away at home several years ago. We are not sure what finally took him but will have fond memories of watching him shuffle along the road below, gripping onto his trusty walking pole and hearing the sound of his gruff voice as he chatted away to Marsella.

Marsella survived for a couple of years after she lost Gabriel, sadly developing dementia. She was moved into a nursing home and passed away a few months later. She was such a robust woman, but old age is a cruel master.

The Citröen Mahari I so loved has gone. We thought one of the family might have kept it, but presume, as we've not seen it since, that it was sold.

Their house was left to its own devices for several years. On a recent visit we found it had finally been sold to a family who will use it as a holiday home. From the amount of detritus building up in the large trailer parked outside, plus the constant drilling, banging and hammering noises emanating from the interior, it seems as though they are well on their way to restoring it. We just hope they do something with the dilapidated chimney and roof!

Richard

Richard's children are now grown and thriving. He has spent many years trying to find someone to settle down with and is currently happy with a lady whose parents own a house in a nearby village. He is as cheerful as ever and is still running his business. We also discovered he plays the flute when we spied a trio of musicians playing beautifully in one of the old town squares. I had to do a double-take when I saw one of them was Richard.

He still asks after our daughter.

Olivier

Olivier is running a successful *Electro/ Ménage* business (electrical and electronic goods, spares, etc.) just outside the village and a large, new transit van which he uses for deliveries. His wife sometimes helps in the shop and their 'little' boy is now a young man.

We spoke to Olivier recently when he delivered a new dishwasher to Gilbert and Annie. He is as chatty and friendly as ever and we are so pleased he's doing well, though we always suspected that, with his work ethic, he was bound to succeed.

Philippe

Philippe's butcher shop is still a thriving business, often with a long queue snaking outside the shop during the high season. His two sons work alongside him with a permanent employee. When it's quiet, Philippe is now able to leave the shop in the hands of his sons and take a day or two off.

Philippe's lovely wife is no longer with us. We found out one summer four years ago. Her cancer had returned after she had been free of it for several years. She died three months after receiving the diagnosis.

We found out when we bounded into Phillipe's shop, full of smiles after just arriving for our holiday. Philippe didn't respond as he always would to our gleeful shouts of *Bonjour!*, simply glancing our way and beckoning to us to come close so he could deliver the awful news quietly and not alert other shoppers. I will always remember him placing a hand over his heart and in English quietly saying, "I am heartbroken. My wife, she is dead." She had died just a few weeks earlier. It was so very sad.

Nowadays, Philippe is back to his old self, calling Rob 'Bobeeeee', still loving the beer we regularly take him from the UK and cheerfully passing the time of day with us when he gets the chance.

The Chimney Sweeps

They are still plying their trade up and down the valley during July and August as we see the van parked in the town from time to time. We haven't seen hide nor hair of Rob's admirer or had a visit from them for the past couple of years, and have no clue as to why. It could be the couple have retired and the business has passed to the son, who may not be quite as diligent as his parents.

Gilbert and Annie

They are still frequent visitors to their house next to ours. We see them more than ever and share *apéritifs* whenever we can.

Gilbert visits their house more often than Annie, often popping up for a couple of days, then travelling back to Cannes. He still likes to go for long bike rides or hikes in the mountains, though admits that he's slowed down a little. He has also taken over the position of *Chef de Commune*, replacing Albert.

They are still the friendliest and most polite people. Both now attend English classes in Cannes and are always keen to practise their language skills whenever they see us. They're doing pretty well, too.

Michel and Sylvanna

They regularly visit their house further up the hillside and are still resident in Nice. Both are now retired and their daughter spent time in Australia. I believe she returned and last we heard, Michel and Sylvanna were now grandparents. We bump into them rarely these days, but whenever we do, it's always good to catch up.

Maxwell The Dog

Our fabulous, funny and amazing little dog succumbed to liver disease a couple of years ago. We were mortified at having to make that dreadful decision pet owners inevitably face and were totally heartbroken. Call us daft, but Max's ashes are stored in a little pewter urn, marked with a paw print and currently rest on the shelf of a bookcase here at home in the UK.

Before he became ill, we were joined by Maisie; another Wire Fox Terrier bought from the same breeder as Maxwell. I think Max was a bit put out with the behaviour of this little minx who liked to chew and drag toilet paper from the roller, and really didn't approve at all. It took a while, but eventually they became firm friends. Maisie's first trip to France was sadly Max's last and he left us only six weeks after returning.

Since Max's demise, Maisie has accompanied us to France regularly and she has now been joined by Teddy, a Fox Terrier too. He was five years old when we adopted him. Due to changes in their circumstances, his family could no longer cope with him. He is a headstrong, boisterous boy and it took a while for Maisie to accept him. To this day, they have the occasional spat. They love their trips to France, are impeccably behaved in hotels and restaurants and love their long walks in the mountains. They are constantly admired by the French we encounter.

Other Dogs

Leika and Angela, Gabriel and Marsella's dogs died a couple of years apart. Angela, by all accounts, wandered off. According to Simone and Albert, some small remains were found eventually. Whether she was attacked and killed or she died of natural causes we'll never know, but a dead animal in the wild becomes food for many. Leika was poisoned and although she was rushed to the vet, he couldn't save her. There was some suspicion that it was carried out deliberately, but we find this difficult to believe. She was never a bothersome animal and our local community are simply not capable. It was more than likely she ingested rat poison on the farm.

Monsieur Le Veterinaire and Anita

Our vet suffered from a brain tumour and the practice closed for a long time following the surgery to remove it. We were really shocked, but happy to know he had recovered and was back treating both the small pets and farm animals in the valley.

A few months later and visiting once again, Anita told us we would have to find another practice as her husband was retiring; his tumour had returned. He treated Maisie and Teddy one final time and we thanked him for his attention to our dogs over the years and wished him well.

Passing by on our summer holiday, the practice appeared to be open again. Anita explained her husband was now seriously ill, unable to walk or talk and it was only a matter of time. Sadly, he passed away in late August 2019. Anita was continuing to work at the surgery as she said it kept her busy, but she was so very heartbroken and admitted life was difficult. She continued to help keep the practice open for a while until the new vet was settled, but sadly left in September 2020.

The New Vet

Our vets fees have now skyrocketed compared to all the years we got away with paying peanuts. However, they are still cheaper than your average UK vet. Our new vet is very outgoing, seems endlessly cheerful and is always up for a banter. With a constant sparkle in the eye, a bucket-load of charm and a slight resemblance to the senior Sean Connery, Rob and I agree he must have acquired quite a fan club amongst his female clients. I haven't told my girlfriends yet!

The Little Restaurant

The lovely little restaurant never re-opened and lies abandoned and run down. We believe that the new road, built to remove the twists and turns of the old route, left the restaurant isolated, unable to benefit from passing traffic. More restaurants have opened in our village thereby limiting the amount of possible clientele. Sadly, the Eau Vive is no longer deemed a viable proposition for budding restaurateurs.

Colmars Les Alpes

Our gorgeous village and its environs were used as a location for a film called, *Jusqu'à ce que la mort nous unisse, Until Death Unites Us,* taken from a book of the same name, and was shown on TV3 in France in November. We have been trying to get our hands on a DVD, but have had no luck finding it yet.

The Old Town remains the same, busiest during the summer months. The market and the Medieval Fête are as popular as ever. New shops and restaurants have appeared and others changed hands.

Our Commune

These days, it is very quiet. Things have changed since our first meeting all those years ago. One property has sold twice and is now a holiday rental, another is for sale. Other properties remain empty for much of the year but often occupied during August and/or February by the original owner's children, all of whom are adults; some of them married with offspring of their own.

Daniel still cuts the grass for the commune and he is now a grandfather. His adult son usually clears the road of snow in winter. Daniel's family still live permanently in the commune and he, his brother and extended family farm extensively. These days they seem to have gone into the goat business judging from the small herd in a field next to the little road. We hope it's for the production of goat's cheese!

Letch's wife still lives just below us, alone. Her grandchildren are now young adults and she gets plenty of visits from her family. She remains as strong as an ox. She also has an allotment, and never sits still. After many years, she still doesn't speak to us, but does smile occasionally.

The Skiing

Our ski resort has had many upgrades, installing more efficient lift systems and a great toboggan run, on rails, that launches children and adults down the steep and twisting track. Throughout summer and winter, much screaming and laughter can be heard as they hurtle down the mountainside.

Plumbing and Satellite

Since Rob installed his gizmo, we have never had a leak. (I hope I'm not tempting fate by saying that!)

The satellite continues to work, except when a storm decides to visit and interrupts the signal.

FRIENDS AND FAMILY

Rosi and Jeff still visit frequently, usually combining their transatlantic trip with a visit to the UK to see family and friends. After Key West, they maintain Colmars les Alpes is their favourite place on earth, and believe me, they've been everywhere! Having said that, they've recently bought an apartment in the Apalachian mountains and I suspect Colmars ranking in their affections will have dropped one notch.

Dickie is still living in Key West and is now in his late 80s. He still paints every evening, setting up his easel in a chosen spot around the old town, but now has to sit rather than stand. His bicycle is now a tricycle.   Unfortunately, he's been diagnosed with Parkinson's disease though, thankfully, it is being managed really well.   He has suffered a bout of skin cancer and suffers with arthritis.   He has just had a major exhibition of his work in Key West of which he was justly very proud.

Bob and Sylviane are retired, though Bob does occasionally carry out a joinery job for a bit of extra cash now and again and does copious amounts of work in his childrens' homes to help them out.   They are grandparents to four, but inherited another two when their son's marriage failed and he settled with a new partner.   We see them every time we go down to our little French house, staying overnight and sometimes for longer.   Bob used his joinery skills to help us rebuild our balcony.

Gill, Georgia and Eve have returned a couple of times to the house and we still manage to take our 'girls' holiday once a year to a variety of cities or resorts around Europe.   Our hubbies are still enthusiastically endorsing this. No idea why...

Elaine and Trevor have stayed several times, the last time during the summer.   Elaine had a serious accident on her horse, six months previously that, she thinks, will prevent her from skiing in the future, but is intending to try.   Trevor is pleased he won't be held responsible for our dog(s) any time soon.

Terry and Janice have also visited many times, but these days, now retired, tend to be occupied with their large garden and their four young grandchildren, though Tez takes time out to play golf. Plans are afoot for another visit soon.

Our family visit often and we love spending time with them. Our little granddaughters are learning to ski and along with our daughter Tasha and partner Dan, join us for February half term for fun in the snow. Our older granddaughter is finding her way in the world after earning her degree. Nikki loves to spend time at the French house and Ben has not been on a snowboard since his accident.

Rob is still working and I confess to urging him to retire sooner rather than later. Of course, he says I'm nagging, but he's now coming around to the idea at last.

We continue to visit our little French home as often as we can, making improvements as and when necessary. We do get away to other far flung places now and again, but our valley, the people and the house will always hold a very special place in our hearts.

... BUT THERE'S MORE

After many months of writing and re-writing after my editor had expertly checked through it, I was happy that my little tale about our early years of owning our French house was finally finished. I was ready to progress to the next stage, but, living through such an extraordinary and terrible event, I felt the need to continue and conclude with one more summer; the summer of 2020.

This book just wouldn't be complete without mentioning the pandemic and Covid19, the virus that has infected the world and caused thousands of deaths, weakened economies and untold misery for millions. No-one has escaped the pressures and difficulties of lockdowns, the uncertainties of the workplace and the anguish of not seeing family and friends. Normal lives have been put on hold. As I write these lines in late summer, 2020, we have begun to see some welcome improvements and freedoms slowly returning, but we're not out of the woods yet, as is evidenced by the precautions we all now have to take.

As travel restrictions gradually eased here in the UK, we were finally able to go to our little French house once more and see how our little community was faring.

This is the story of our recent return to France, with the virus playing a minor supporting role.

Bonus Chapter 31
COVID AND CAMPING

We used to cover the miles to our French house with just one overnight stop, but nowadays we take our time, relax rather than panic, chill rather than rush. As soon as France and the UK dropped their 'tit-for-tat' quarantine measures for travellers, we couldn't wait to get away and rapidly booked the Tunnel and a couple of nights in hotels for the outward and homeward journeys, ensuring all were 'Covid safe'. We also planned to relive the past and spend a week 'under canvas.' Our friends thought we were losing it, "What! Really?" Our 'kids' had a different viewpoint, "Brilliant, do it!" We thought "Why not?"

Having spent years camping all over France with our growing children, we were happy to know the tradition was continuing with our daughter. She, her partner and our two small granddaughters were camping on an enormous site near Ramatuelle and the beach of Pampelonne. Never having quite lost the camping bug, we both decided it might a good idea to take a week away from our little home in the mountains and join them.

After some research in the UK, we were amazed at how things had moved forward since we'd been the proud owners of a large tent which weighed half a ton, along with a huge bag of heavy-weight poles to support it. The only way to take this bulky mass of canvas and metal anywhere was to use a trailer, dragging it through forests and fields, over mountain passes and onto numerous ferries and hovercrafts - remember those? On one occasion, it sped off on its own when Tez, who had been following behind in his car, failed to notice we were approaching a speed bump and had to brake suddenly at the last minute. The result of this minor collision somehow dislodged the trailer from its coupling and it flew passed us, continuing along the road until it finally came to rest in a hedge!

Once on the campsite, it used to take forever to erect the tent. First, we struggled to match one pole to another, then risked hernias attempting to heave the canvas into place. It could get a little fraught on occasions.

"What are you doing?" Rob would enquire

"What do you mean? I'm doing what you asked me?"

"No you're not. You're doing it all wrong."

"OK, Mr Know-It-All. You do it if you're so bloody clever!"

Meanwhile, our young children were impatiently skipping about yelling they wanted to go in the pool. To distract them while we continued to struggle, we usually sent them on a mission to find the showers and toilets, only for them to return a couple of minutes later after locating the pool instead and driving us mad with their continued pleas.

Strangely, Rob and I have always been quite nostalgic when recalling those halcyon holidays when the sun always shone and our children were little. But the mind has a way of placing a soft filter over the more irksome memories, such as erecting or collapsing the tent in the rain, or attempting to sleep on an inflatable mattress that took half an hour to inflate with a foot pump, then bounced you around like a rubber ball every time one of you turned over.

Thanks to modern technology, this was all in the past. Within a week, operating in our usual impulsive manner, we'd purchased a modern Airbeam tent. For quite a largish tent, it only took one man ten minutes to erect, they said, folded to a reasonably manageable size and fitted in the back of our decade-old Discovery, leaving some room to spare for the rest of the paraphernalia campers require. A self-inflating mattress was also purchased. (Deflating and fitting it back into its storage bag was a whole different ball game, but that's another story.) We then fished about in the loft and retrieved useful camping accessories we'd not been near in more than twenty years!

With the car packed to the roof and the dogs, Teddy and Maisie, secured on the back seat, we set off to the Tunnel. A one-way system was in operation in the terminal building, the duty-free shop had closed and apparently, it appeared food outlets only opened one at a time, but offered to deliver cold food and drink to your car for those who were reluctant to enter the main building. It felt quite alien seeing everyone walking around in masks and was very quiet inside, even though the car parks were relatively full.

Forbidden to leave our cars once on the train, with toilets off limits and closed, I made sure I went beforehand! I felt only a tiny bit sorry for those who had chosen to ignore the announcement in the belief it didn't apply to them, and a little smug as I caught sight of them making their way towards relief and finding none.

We enjoyed our stays in the two overnight hotels I'd booked. Safe and clean with socially-distanced tables in the restaurants and masks worn by staff and visitors. We saw notices that services along the *autoroute* also warned of the obligatory wearing of masks upon entry. Initially, when leaving the car or venturing out of a hotel room, we never gave masks a second thought. It took a while for the brain to catch up to the fact that '*things ain't what they used to be'* and often we'd find one or the other of us dashing back to retrieve them. It wasn't long before grabbing them became habitual, but I would still remind Rob, just in case, or fly into a blind panic if I couldn't find one.

Arriving at the house to find all was well, we unpacked what we needed, but simply couldn't face removing all the camping gear. Getting it stored out of the way would mean trying to get the large tent bag up the spiral staircase to put in one of unoccupied bedrooms, only to have to drag it back down again a week later. Not an easy task, so it languished in the car with the rest of the gear.

Our first week in the mountains disappeared so quickly it was almost as if we'd climbed into the Tardis just after arrival and set the controls to land us back in the same place a week into the future. They say (whoever 'they' are) that time travels more quickly the older you get and I can guarantee it's true. If it speeds up anymore, we'll be back before we left! No sooner than I'd unpacked clothing from our bags it seemed I was packing the same bags for our departure.

"I don't know why you pack so much. You never wear it all anyway," says Rob.

"That's because I need to cater for every eventuality." I reply, defensively.

"Like what? You're staying in a little village in the mountains and a week in a tent, not in some posh hotel in Monaco!"

I resisted the urge to remind him about the number of short-sleeved shirts, tee shirts and shorts he'd bought along.

We left around midday after spending the morning making sure we'd got everything a camper would need and saying '*Au revoir*' to Gilbert and Annie who, I'm sure, thought we were bonkers. As two residents of Cannes, they were in the mountains escaping the crowds and heat, and there we were, heading the other way.

It was a pleasant drive to the campsite, except for the final few miles, where the notorious Côte d'Azur summer traffic was moving at a snail's pace. Those on scooters and motorbikes were the exception, clad in shorts and tees, speeding towards us hell bent on ending their lives as they crossed white lines and dodged in and out of vehicles with hardly room to spare.

Leaving behind the exhaust fumes and the stresses of kamikaze youth, we continued along a meandering road passing through vineyards which stretched away into the distance. A tiny, white roadside chalet offering *dégustations* was our landmark before turning left into a lane leading to the campsite. Our first impressions were really favourable. A beautiful oleander tree bursting with bright pink blooms, stood guard at the entrance; fields of vines surrounded the site. Leaving the sanctuary of our air-conditioned car to check-in, we gasped as the heat smacked us in the face.

Bloody hell, who opened the oven door!" Rob exclaimed.

Masked up as instructed, we confirmed our booking at the tiny reception desk, were given wrist bands, a gizmo to open the barrier and the number of the pitch we'd been allocated.

"It has got shade hasn't it?" I asked, checking they'd read my booking request.

"*Bien sûr*. There are lots of trees," came the reply.

Entering the site, we could see mature trees and more flowering shrubs bordering the tiny one-way road that wended its way around it, going sharply uphill before plunging back down to level terrain near the entrance. Most of the pitches, it seemed, contained holiday chalets arranged on terraces with high hedges providing privacy. Only a few provided for pitching tents. Caravans and motorhomes were noticeable by their absence, thankfully. We were really pleased. It all looked so pretty and well-tended.

Things started well. The pitch we were given had several large trees to provide much-needed shade, but our situation started to go rapidly downhill about half an hour later as we discovered the pitch was too small for our tent! Rob and I had tried every which way to make it fit, laying the protective ground sheet horizontally across the space, turning it vertically, then diagonally, dragging it a metre one way then the other.

We hadn't a hope in hell, nor had we given thought to the added impossibility of parking the car within the space too. The dogs watched our antics from their spot anchored to a couple of small tree trunks, no doubt wishing we'd get on with it as they needed a walk.

So, masks on, hot, dusty, weary and very, very sweaty, we returned to Reception begging the proprietor for another pitch. He'd misread the measurements I'd sent him, hence our struggles to fit a quart into a pint pot.

Things then hit rock bottom when the proprietor explained there were no other pitches free. The region was very busy, all other sites were full and so were the hotels, the only thing he could offer was a suitably sized pitch that would be available the next morning. Sitting on a wall back in the shade of the unwanted pitch, with the dogs panting like steam trains in the heat, we discussed our options. Our only solution was to spend the night in the car. We solemnly delivered this news to the proprietor who, along with his wife, had come up with their own solution and offered us free accommodation in a vacant rental chalet for the night. Our relief was tangible. I couldn't stop saying 'Merci', forgetting it was their fault in the first place.

An hour or two later, after we'd stepped into air conditioned, Covid-secure heaven, had showers, dressed in clean clothes, glugged a cold beer, we were revived and happily tucked into pizza and local rosé wine at the tiny outdoor restaurant. With the sun setting, we finally took the dogs for their evening constitutional, meandering through the vines as they bounded ahead, happy to be outdoors at last, enjoying the cooler air. We stood for a while, admiring the views across the vines, which drew the eye towards the distant hills and the stunning sky, ablaze with colour as the sun gradually sank out of sight.

After sleeping like babies, we took our time leaving the comfort of the accommodation, especially as we had to wait for the new pitch to become vacant. It was a long wait. The occupants were clearly in no hurry to leave even though they noticed my frequent spying missions to check on their progress. I made several visits throughout the morning, gloomily reporting back to Rob that they seemed to be relaxing in their chairs, oblivious to the fact that we were desperate to get our tent up before the sun was at its zenith. It wasn't until midday before they'd packed up and gone.

We made our way to the patch of dusty earth that would be our home for the week. With the sun burning holes in our heads and a tent we'd never had out of the bag, we realised we were in for an uncomfortable time. A lone baby tree whose feeble shadow was about the diameter of your average dustbin lid, provided the only shade. With the engine running and the air con blowing, we left the dogs in the car while we proceeded to get the tent up in ten minutes. We could hardly believe that the advertising bumph actually told the truth! Just another hour or so and everything else was unloaded from the car into what by now was a six by three metre oven! By the time we'd finished, we were back to being disgustingly grimy with sweat dripping off us in rivulets. All we wanted now was a cool shower, the opportunity to drink a gallon of cold water and get some relief from the searing heat. Finally, our tasks completed and the car parked on the pitch, we stood back and saw we were left with a meagre square metre or so of dusty space to set up our table and chairs!

Camping means sharing intimate spaces like shower and toilet blocks with others, but with our brains about to be cooked and all common sense on the run, worries about Covid security had flown out of the window along with concerns about sharing such spaces with people from God knows where, flinging virus particles all over the place! Although we'd kept the dogs hydrated with bowlfuls of cold water – we had electricity and rented a full-sized fridge from the site - they were looking very forlorn lying limply in the dust. It was obvious we were not the only ones in need of a cool down. Taking it in turns, we both took a dog and put them in the shower cubicle with us, making sure they had a thorough soaking. Not sure if it was against the rules or not, but we were past caring.

Later, showered and feeling a lot cooler in the shade, kindly provided by high hedges blocking the sun's rays as it slipped towards the horizon, we finally felt relaxed and happy and above all, safe, even though the news reports stated there had been a worrying increase in infection rates along the Côte d'Azur. Having observed the rigorous attention to mask-wearing and cleaning, we were optimistic that the protocols were being followed. Logic dictated that the site owners certainly wouldn't welcome any outbreaks resulting in closure of the site. We were impressed to see shower and toilet blocks were thoroughly cleaned several times a day, with the aroma from antiseptic fluid always present in the air. Outside each entryway, a sanitiser was available from a dispenser, and in each toilet cubicle, a bottle of the same was provided to spray the toilet seat after use. We also watched one evening as the staff set up audience seating in the car park in preparation for a children's entertainer. Positioned a metre apart, each chair was then thoroughly cleaned with sanitiser.

We quickly sussed out the times of day when the tent did its impression of a furnace, so made sure we were nowhere near it. We couldn't use the campsite pool for long periods as dogs were rightly barred. As it was forbidden to leave them unsupervised, it meant we had to go for a swim one at a time, abandoning the other to slowly bake on the pitch with the dogs, or sit on a wall somewhere in the shade, bored witless. We did ask nicely if we could use a fenced off area, well away from pool and sunbathers, in deep shade with seats provided for the smokers who had to use it, but the answer was still *Non*!

So, we set off to Pampelonne beach, dog-friendly with a wonderful breeze blowing off the sea. It meant driving and paying a small fee to park for the day, in full sun, heating the car enough to roast a Sunday joint on the dashboard. Only the *Tikki Club* crowd could afford the 'Valet Parking Only' shelters, with shade for their Bentleys, Ferraris and Aston Martins.

On our first visit to Pampelonne, we sauntered towards the beach, armed to the teeth with everything we'd need for ourselves and our dogs to enjoy a day on the sand. We paused alongside the *Tikki Club*, its restaurant housed in a typical looking beachside building, all straw roofs and bamboo, and scanned the lunch menu wondering if we might be able to grab an affordable salad. It was possible if you were willing to part with around 100 euros, 250 if you wanted lobster with it!

Obviously, it catered for the unimaginably wealthy whom we later spied being transported there on launches from their superyachts anchored offshore.

Pampelonne beach thankfully failed to mirror the overcrowded beaches recently seen in the UK where people were close enough to lick a stranger's ice cream without moving. At five kilometres long, with soft fine sand, we could see that this beach had only a light sprinkling of humanity, accompanied by their colourful beach parasols flapping in the breeze. Most people seemed to have set up within a couple of metres of the breaking waves and each other, leaving huge swathes of totally empty beach behind them. Obviously, they were not keen on walking far to get their toes wet.

We settled ourselves near a wooden fence, the type that has palings and fence wire. A notice explained the area was planted with beach grass to stabilise and protect the dunes from damage. We secured the dogs to it on long leads and set up camp. They happily settled themselves on their blanket in the shade of the parasol, their noses poking out of the side, gently buffeted by the breeze, keeping them comfortably cool. Rob plonked himself on his towel, lying half in and half out of the shade while I made for the sea and a refreshing swim.

Teddy adores the water. Observing me making my entrance into the sea, he frantically tried to join in and was in danger of uprooting the fence and dragging it across the sand. Rob grabbed the lead before chaos ensued and granted Teddy's desire to get into the water and swim in circles, while I collected Maisie, who was happy to stand and watch. Half an hour later, Teddy had swum the dog equivalent of a watery marathon, and Maisie had exhausted herself running away from the breaking waves and barking at Teddy. We were returning to our patch when a rather worrying noise emanated from Teddy's back end. Rob just managed to get out of the way in time as the reason for the noise became evident, shooting in a stream like water from a firehose. With several metres between us and our nearest neighbour, luckily no-one was on the receiving end, though I'm sure half the beach heard it. I thrust a doggie-bag at Rob, who, courageously and without gagging, picked it up along with several kilos of sand. I was dispatched to put it in a bin.

The remainder of our week flew by with thankfully no repeats of Teddy's high velocity bowel movement. We'd managed not to expire in the heat, had slept well as the night temperatures cooled and loved spending time with our family, enjoying meals out in Ramatuelle, the stunning little village perched high in the hills. We were able to grant our little granddaughters' wishes to stay with us and the dogs for a night, snuggling down together as darkness fell. We even enjoyed popping down to Géant, the huge hypermarket which had become our regular shopping spot, sauntering around in air-conditioned heaven, drooling over the food on offer. Masks on, of course.

When our final morning dawned, we were up early to pack away. The first task had been for the two of us to go into battle with the self-inflating mattress so we could roll it and get it into the bag. It was a wrestling match, with me fully prostrate, opening the valves to let some air out as Rob rolled the thing up. Trouble is, you can't leave the valves open as it re-inflates itself, so I had to close them again, shuffle along on my stomach like a seal, open them again pushing more air out as I did so, while Rob made another turn in the rolling up process.

The tent came down easily and only took time because we couldn't figure out which way to fold it to get it back into its bag. The instructions were about as useful as a chocolate fireguard, so we gave in to 'initiative', which failed on the first attempt, but won out on the second.   With everything finally tossed untidily into the car, the two of us showered, the dogs settled on the back seat, securely fastened into their doggie seat belts, we headed back to the mountains where we could walk in the sunshine without melting like butter.

Our route back took us along the coast towards St. Maxime and then headed inland following the road that gradually spiralled upwards towards hills lined with umbrella pines and tiny villages with enviable views towards the distant Mediterranean. As we continued on, distant hills morphed into mountains and pines into fir and spruce; we were finally back on familiar territory.   Arriving at the house, the sun still shining, we found our son, Ben, already settled in after travelling from the UK on his motorbike. He was spending the week with us and between periods of relaxation and repairing bits on his bike, he'd disappear off for the day, exploring mountain passes and heading over *cols*. The area in which our house sits is a magnet for bikers who love the hairpin bends and Ben was no different, but I was always relieved to hear the bike approaching as he safely arrived back with us.

When he headed home, he left most of his belongings with us to transport back to the UK, along with a bulky present he'd bought for Nikki, his partner, probably to assuage his guilt as she couldn't accompany him on this break because of work commitments. Mum and dad to the rescue again!

Believe it or not, despite all the inconveniences and searing heat we encountered on our return to camping, it hasn't put us off. We're determined to do it again next year ... when it's cooler!

OUR COMMUNITY

With the onset of the pandemic, we often wondered how our little community in Colmars les Alpes was managing. During our time there this summer, we had the opportunity to find out.

Colmars les Alpes

Being a rural area, the valley experienced the loosening of restrictions in larger steps than the more populated areas of France. Life started normalising quite quickly once the process began. However, strict rules still apply with regard to social distancing and mask wearing. Elbow bumping is preferable to hand shaking and the lovely custom of kissing cheeks has ceased for the time being, except among family members. I now say *bisous*, (kisses) while air-kissing from about a metre away.

The Provençal market was permitted to recommence in early July, on Tuesday and Friday mornings, as usual. Disappointingly, one or two of the more regular stalls were missing, including one of our favourites. We missed buying a fat wedge of delicious *Tomme de Montagne*, cut from one of the huge wheels of cheese brought directly from the farm on the road to Lac d'Allos, that were always stacked side by side on an old wooden table. Nevertheless, with several other cheese stalls in attendance selling *Compte*, *Abondance*, *Beaufort* and gorgeous, creamy goats' cheeses, to name but a few, we were happily spoiled and spent a small fortune on enough cheese to stock a small shop. It lasted our entire stay!

A new and novel development, whether dreamt up in light of the Coronavirus or not, was to be found in the old town. Loudspeakers had been installed that were operated from the Tourist Information Office. On market day, they were used to remind people about the importance of wearing masks in the narrow streets and in all shops. They also announced details of any special events happening in the forthcoming few days. It was a useful resource, but we were very happy that it remained silent most of the time and the temptation to subject residents and tourists to non-stop background music had been resisted.

Although there had not been one single case of Coronavirus within the valley and the wider area, residents and tourists of all ages appeared to be obeying the rules diligently. We were most heartened to see this and happy to know that the townsfolk had remained safe and well and hope they continue to do so.

Gilbert

Gilbert was unfortunately (or fortunately depending on your point of view) in his mountain home when the French Government invoked lockdown. He was the only resident of the *copropriété* in residence and spent many weeks holed up alone, but was completely at ease with this. He'd kept himself busy. We benefitted from his labours, finding a pile of neatly sawn wood placed near our log pile, the result of Gilbert finally getting rid of an old set of wooden steps. They led nowhere and as they'd never been in anyone's way, being tucked away on a high bank leaning against a wall, they'd been there for years. With lots of time on his hands, Gilbert decided to make use of them by sawing them into small log-sized pieces and sharing the spoils with his neighbours. He also killed time hiking in the mountains, never encountering a single soul and took to his bicycle for exhilarating rides along totally deserted roads. His mobile phone signal improved too!

Philippe

He took full opportunity of lockdown by having his shop totally refitted, giving himself and his staff more room while reducing customer queueing space a little. Not a problem as long queues always stretch outside on a busy day and social distancing makes little difference to this. Everything looked sleek and very upmarket. Meat and other deli items were beautifully arranged in shiny display cases, cured hams hung regimentally, suspended from a rail fixed to the ceiling. Bottles and jars of delicious sauces and other delights were stored neatly on shelves by the entrance door. The décor had a deep wine-coloured theme and the staff wore a uniform of black t-shirts and long aprons of the same colour. We were very impressed the first time we saw it and Philippe was equally impressed with Rob's facemask! Spying him waiting outside, Philippe pointed and loudly shouted 'Pirate!" This resulted in all the queueing customers turning to see if Johnny Depp had suddenly appeared only to see Rob, in his very bright, pirate-adorned facemask lingering outside minding his own business! A good laugh was had by all.

Olivier

Let me introduce another Olivier. You've not met him yet, but he's another, younger entrepreneur we've come to know over more recent years. We originally became acquainted with him when he ran the 'Cave de Vin', a tiny dark shop buried within the walls of the old town. He then appeared one winter working in a bar on the ski slopes and the following year, at the ice rink. A small restaurant situated in the old town, which has seen itself mothballed from time to time as proprietors came and went, opened again with Olivier at the helm. Over the past few years, this little eatery, serving excellent unfussy food made from locally sourced ingredients, has done extremely well, much of it down to Olivier's bonhomie as he moves through the clientele chatting cheerfully and taking orders. He opens around Easter time and continues through to the end of October, so we always tend to be there in the summer when everyone eats at tables squeezed together, rather haphazardly, outside in the tiny square. A few paces from the restaurant, naturally pure water for the tables is taken directly from a tap in the wall that flows into a stone trough.

In order to comply with Covid protocols, there are now

fewer tables, not that there were many to start with, in order to create sufficient space between them, and masks were being worn by all staff. We arrived one sunny lunchtime, with dogs in tow, in need of a good meal. With all tables fully occupied, we thought we were out of luck, but after a pause, Olivier grabbed an unused table lying against the wall, unfolded it and placed it in a very narrow side street just off the square. Dismissing my worries that we might be mowed down by a cyclist or small vehicle, Olivier assured us we'd be fine. We stuck out like sore thumbs, sitting away from the rest of the diners by some distance, but felt a little less like lepers when another table for two was set up for a young couple a few feet away from us further down the street. They appeared to spend more time practising mouth-to-mouth resuscitation while groping for a pulse than eating! I smiled at the passion of young love, wistfully recalling the days when Rob and I first met. Rob was more interested in the fact that Olivier owned a Harley.

With our return hotels booked, the house thoroughly cleaned and drained of water, we headed back to the UK, where the Government had announced France was to be removed from the "safe list", so that anyone returning after the deadline would be quarantined. As this was announced at 11.15 pm in the UK (12.15 am in France), we knew nothing of it until we received a text from a friend the following morning, just as we were leaving. With no chance of getting back before the deadline, we just had to accept our fate. So, here I am, concluding this book while under strict quarantine for two weeks. *C'est la vie!*

ABOUT THE AUTHOR

Jane was born in Birmingham, and remains a Brummie at heart although she has lived in north Worcestershire for many years. She worked as a lecturer at a college in the West Midlands for most of her career, starting out teaching secretarial subjects and having to re-educate herself every few years as technology and computers gradually took over. By the end of her career, she held the position of Senior Teacher and lecturer in IT. She also has qualifications in photography and fitness instruction, the latter she no longer uses, saying she much prefers being a participant rather than the teacher. Happily married, she and her husband Rob have two children, three granddaughters and two fox terriers. They share their time between the UK and their little house in the Alpes de Haute Provence.